Score Better
At
Trap and Skeet

Score Better
At
Trap and Skeet

Fred Missildine
with
Nick Karas

Stoeger Publishing Company

Library of Congress Cataloging in Publication Data

Missildine, Fred.
  Score better at trap and skeet.

  (Stoeger sportsman's library)
  Reprint of Score better at trap and Score better
at skeet published by Winchester Press, New York,
in 1971 and 1972, respectively.
  1. Trap-shooting. I. Karas, Nicholas, joint
author. II. Karas, Nicholas. Score better at
skeet. 1977. III. Title.
GV1181.M5   1977   799.3'13   77-8793
ISBN 0-88317-043-4

First Stoeger quality paperback edition, September 1977
Second printing, August 1979

This Stoeger Sportsman's Library edition is published by
arrangement with Winchester Press

Distributed to the book trade by Follett Publishing Company
and to the sporting goods trade by Stoeger Industries.
In Canada distributed to the book trade and sporting goods
trade by Stoeger Trading Company, 2020R 32nd Avenue,
Northeast, Calgary, Alberta T2E 6T4

Printed in the United States of America

Introduction

Of all the shooting games that men have come up with since firearms were invented, trap and skeet clearly belong at the top of the list. Both were originally devised to improve field shooting and/or provide practice for the shotgunner when game was unavailable. Both still fulfill those functions, but also go far beyond them. In fact, both have developed into exacting and exciting disciplines in their own right.

As these sports have developed, they have become both more complex and more interesting. And they often pose problems for shooters—problems that sometimes call for help. This can be forthcoming on the range simply by asking a good shooting instructor what's going wrong. I have been known to do this myself—and if you see me at the range and have a problem, don't hesitate to ask. Another approach is to find a book that will tell you how to improve your shooting. Unfortunately, this hasn't always worked out so well, because so many of these books do one of two things: Either they get so bogged down with ballistics, exceptions, and technical nicities that the poor confused shooter decides he'll never figure it all out and takes up some other sport—or they explain which end of the gun goes off, give enough safety advice to keep the shooter from getting into trouble, and then say farewell and leave him to learn the rest of the game for himself.

Well, I planned this book to change all that. What I wanted was a book that would give the beginner what he needs and yet also help the experienced shooter—the fellow who just can't quite get those last few targets he needs to move from Class B, say, to A, or from A to AA. If you're already an AA shooter, you don't need this book (of course, I'd be delighted if you'd buy it anyway and give it to someone who does); but if you're a rank beginner or even a Class B or Class A shooter, there's still room for you to improve. And improvement doesn't just mean shooting higher scores—it also means shooting with less effort and enjoying it more. Too many people have learned to shoot without learning *how* to shoot. Some even win before they've learned how to win, but they can't do it consistently.

Drawing on thirty years of experience, not only as a tournament shooter but also as an industry professional and shooting instructor, I have tried to reduce trap and skeet to their true fundamentals, stressing those things that are the foundation of all great shooting. Shooting high scores and winning depend on a combination of many things, but once the fundamentals have been mastered, shooting success is mostly a question of gun fit, practice, and concentration.

I'm a lot handier with a shotgun than with a pen, but I've tried to put this all down on paper as simply as possible in the following pages, for your benefit. If it helps you hit a few more of the targets you've been missing, break the ones you've been breaking a little cleaner, and enjoy the whole game a bit more, the struggle will have been worth it.

Fred Missildine

Score Better
At Trap

Dedication

To my young son Mark,
who, I hope,
may someday take up
where I leave off.

Foreword

I've been privileged to know Fred Missildine for many years, even though his long professional association with Winchester ended before mine commenced. He's a fine gentleman and a superb all-around wing shot who can hit just about anything that flies, and do it consistently. His skeet record speaks for itself, and nobody who saw him break 200 straight to win the Grand American Professional Class Championship, and then add the Handicap and High Over All, would ever underestimate him as a trapshooter. Even rarer than these attributes, however, is the fact that Fred is a born teacher who can get some of his skill to "rub off" on his pupils. Between his relationship with the Sea Island and Lake Placid Clubs, his years as a Winchester professional and his wartime stint teaching fighter pilots, Fred has coached literally thousands of shooters. He's worked with every kind of shooter from the so-called "helpless" cases to established tournament stars, and there are darned few shooters who don't have something to learn from him.

This is especially true today, for tournament trap seems to get tougher every year. Tournaments that used to be won with scores in the 90s and 190s now need straights, and straights in the shoot-off, too. The only way to keep pace, even if you're a top shooter, is to break another target or two, out of every hundred, that you used to miss. In *Score Better at Trap*, Fred shows you how!

NED LILLY

Contents

Introduction

Ever since guns were first invented, men have written books trying to tell other men how to shoot them. It hasn't always worked, though, because so many of these books do one of two things: either they get so bogged down with ballistics, exceptions and technicalities that the poor confused shooter decides he'll never figure it all out, and takes up some other sport—or they explain which end of the gun goes off, give enough safety advice to keep the shooter from blowing himself up and then say farewell and leave him to learn the rest of the game for himself.

Hundreds of books have been written for the beginner, but few have tried to help the more experienced shooter—the fellow who wants more than anything to be another Orlich, Devers or Riegger, but can't get those last few targets he needs to move up from Class B to A, or from A to AA. It was mostly with this fellow in mind that this book was written. If you're already an AA shooter, you don't need this book (of course, I'd be delighted if you'd buy it anyway, and give it to someone who does) ; but if you're a Class A shooter, there's still room for you to improve. And improvement doesn't just mean shooting higher scores—it also means shooting with less effort and enjoying it more. Too many people have learned to shoot without learning how to shoot. Some even win before they've learned how to win, but they can't do it consistently.

Drawing on thirty years of experience, not only as a tournament shooter but also as an industry professional and shooting instructor, I have tried to reduce the game of trapshooting to its true fundamentals, stressing those things that are the foundation of all great trapshooting. Shooting high scores and winning depend on a combination of many things, but once the fundamentals have bee mastered, the game is mostly a question of gun fit, practice and concentration.

I'm a lot handier with a shotgun than with a pen, but I've tried to put this all down on paper as simply as possible in the following pages, for your benefit. If it helps you hit a few more of the targets you've been missing, break the ones you've been breaking a little cleaner and enjoy the whole game a bit more, the struggle will have been worth it.

FRED MISSILDINE

A Word To
Left-Handed Shooters

Trapshooting is a fine game for left-handers, for though it's no advantage, it's not the slightest disadvantage, either. This book was written from the point of view of a right-handed shooter, which is what I am, and obviously what I've said has to be turned around in order to make it apply to portsiders. I suspect that most lefties have long since learned how to translate right-handed instructions for themselves, and are probably sick to death of being told to do so. Accordingly, I've mostly left you on your own in the following pages.

F.M.

Score Better
At Trap

The Trapshooting Game & How It Started

Trapshooting is a tantalizing game. It's a simple game to pick up—deceptively simple—for the rules are easy to learn, and almost any man, woman or child can break at least a few targets the very first time he or she tries. It's a game that can endure for your whole lifetime, and fine scores are returned every year by shooters in their early teens and others in their eighties. It's a game in which shooters of varying degrees of experience and skill can participate enjoyably together, thanks to the handicap system. But it's also a game you can never master completely, and thus a constant challenge.

Actually, of course, trapshooting is three games. There is singles trap, at 16-yard rise, which is the basic form of the game. In this form, the shooter takes five shots at each of five different "pegs," or stations, at clay targets which are thrown at constantly variable angles by a mechanical trap located 16 yards in front of him. In handicap trap, everything is the same except that the shooter moves back, as far as 27 yards from the trap house, in the case of the maximum handicap. And finally, there is trap doubles, in which the shooter shoots from each of the five stations at pairs of targets, thrown simultaneously but at predetermined angles. These three games combine to form a fiercely competitive sport that continues to grow in the United States at a rate of about ten percent a year, judging from clay-bird sales, and which now involves more than forty thousand serious shooters, not to mention a much larger number of more casual competitors. Yes, it's a great sport, and many shooters think it's more than that—they think it's something of an art as well.

In the beginning, trapshooting was only considered an adjunct to or substitute for field shooting. When it was first introduced into the United States, it was practiced almost entirely by hunters who wanted to maintain or improve their shooting skills between gunning seasons. Some hunters still shoot trap in the off-season, but the sport has such high intrinsic values that many shooters come to prefer the trap peg to the field, and concentrate exclusively on this sport the year around. Today, fewer than half of the registered trap shooters are also active hunters.

Knowing something about the origin and development of trapshooting won't help you break any more targets when you step to the line, but it's still an interesting story. If you think it's hard to break a hundred straight now, you ought to consider how hard it was back before we had plastic shot collars, electric traps, and targets that almost break from the backwash of a near miss. Just so that we won't be total strangers when we do start working on your game, let me tell you a few things about the game of trapshooting that you probably never knew.

Trapshooting as we know it today is relatively modern, tracing only to about 1880 or 1890. Even though some form of "trapshooting" existed for more than a hundred years prior to this date, the game as we recognize it had to wait for the development of modern targets, traps and shotguns. Otherwise, it could never have reached its present efficient state and come to provide the contest it now does.

How did it start? There are several theories. The commonest one attributes it to some discontented Englishmen who were deprived of the right to hunt wild game because it all belonged to the king and his royal followers. As a substitute, they devised a shooting game that simulated gunning in the wild, and used live birds as the targets.

The earliest written record of trapshooting, historians tell us, is found in the English publication *The Sporting Magazine*. As issue of 1793 mentions the "increasing prevalence" of the game and that ". . . it has already been established for some time."

An area just outside of London, near Ealing, was one of the early trapshooting sites. It's called Old Hats. The name supposedly derived from the method shooters first used to release the birds. The traps were nothing more than a hole in the ground, with an old hat placed over the bird and hole. When it came time for a shot, the hat was simply kicked off the hole and the escaping bird shot.

Gradually more sophisticated trapshooting became prevalent in the early 1800's. At the House Pigeon Club near Hornsey Wood, for example, the traps were wooden boxes sunk into the ground at five positions. One shooter took his turn at a time and when he called for a pull, the trap boy would yank a cord attached to a sliding lid on the box and the bird would burst free. Quite a variety of game was used in the traps, ranging from wild and domestic pigeons to sparrows and even quail. The larger pigeons, however, proved most popular whenever they could easily be obtained.

The English sense of gamesmanship took trapshooting a step further with the formation of another club, the "High Hats," in 1832. High hats were used in the shoot, and covered a pigeon in a hole. Whenever the referee called "shoot," the gunners would lean over and pick up the hat, releasing the bird. However, the shooter had to place the hat on his head before he could take aim and fire!

Trapshooting came to the United States early in the 19th century. The first formal trapshoots of which we have a record were held in Cincinnati, Ohio, by the Sportmen's Club, beginning in 1831. Of course, the clay target hadn't yet been invented, so the traps were loaded with live birds. Domesticated pigeons weren't quite as plentiful as in England, but the then prolific passenger pigeon made a good substitute. Nine years after the Cincinnati club was formed, a Long Island club was established, and the following year, the New York Sportsmen's Club added trapshooting to its activities. The sport was well received in this country and grew rapidly. Most contests were held as matches between individuals rather

**Shooting live pigeons
at Hornsey Wood, near London,
in the early 1800s.**

than among clubs because of the unpredictable nature of the target and the lack of uniform rules for the game.

The 1850's were the real heyday of live pigeon shooting, but even then, there were stirrings of things to come. Many people resented the killing of live birds as targets and saw little sport in the game. To begin with, all the birds didn't fly the same and some pullers didn't pull as well as others. Many good men were "beaten" because the system wasn't efficient or consistent enough to give everyone an equal chance. Then, too, live pigeons in the wild were becoming harder to find and the passenger pigeon was being killed off by excessive harvesting.

Charles Portlock of Boston was one of the key figures in the trend away from live birds. In 1866, he introduced the first glass balls that could be used as trap targets and a trap to throw them. This was the inauguration of what might be called the glass-ball period of trapshooting. Many of the professionals who had made their reputation by shooting live targets resented the glass-ball shoots and at first tried to shun them. However, up and coming shooters took to the balls as if live birds were going out of business—which in fact they were.

Several states passed laws forbidding live-bird shoots, and this did a lot to spur on the glass-ball shooting. But even these targets weren't the answer that trapshooting needed. The traps used to throw the balls were imperfect and didn't always function the same. The balls themselves had some drawbacks. Broken glass wasn't the only one; some balls were so hard that a full load of shot at close range couldn't break them. Variations on the glass balls were legion. Some inventors attached feathers

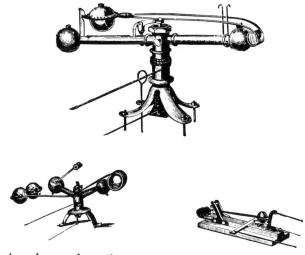

Various forms of rotating
and stationary glass-ball traps
in use around 1870.

on the outside to simulate live birds while others stuffed
feathers inside; when a ball was broken, the feathers flew.
Other ingenious makers added powder to the balls, which
broke with a puff of smoke when hit, while still others
added powders that would flash when broken.

One of the famous shooters of the era was Capt.
A. H. Bogardus. He had been a famous wing shot and
market hunter long before he faced his first trap but
easily made the transition. He also helped the glass-ball
business with his exhibition shooting prowess, and further
advanced it by inventing his own roughed glass ball in
1876. Better yet, he built a better trap to throw them. It
was simple, inexpensive and threw targets in a consistent
flight path.

Even at their best, however, glass balls lacked
a lot as targets for trapshooting, and since this was a great
age for inventors, a score of ingenious men rose to the
challenge with other ideas, every bit as varied as the
glass balls. One was a balloon encased in a cardboard
disc that made it look like a miniature model of the
planet Saturn. Another, introduced by G. F. Kolb, a
Philadelphia naturalist and conservationist, resembled
a real bird. It was a bird-shaped bit of stiff paper attached

Shooting over Bogardus's
glass-ball traps, about 1880.

to a wire ball. Uniquely, the wire ball could be launched from any of the glass-ball traps in use at the time. What's more, it was reusable and left little room for argument. If someone doubted that the bird was hit, all you had to do was find it and show where the shot pellets had passed through. Mark them, and the bird was almost as good as new. The balls were practically everlasting, according to Kolb. For all of this, they were never widely adopted.

The year 1880 marked a major turning point in trapshooting for it was the year in which a new target was introduced which was ultimately to create the game as we know it today. Prior to 1880, there were few organized trap clubs. Most of the shooting was in exhibition matches between real hotshots, men like Bogardus, Cozens, Carver and Long. Average shooters never had a chance to develop their skill. Standardization of traps and targets was almost impossible. What the game needed was a real technological breakthrough. That's what George Ligowsky did for it.

This Cincinnati shooter used to spend his summers at the seashore. One day, so the story goes, he was watching a group of boys skipping flat stones over the water and was impressed by the way they soared, in a flat trajectory. He immediately realized the application to trapshooting and that same year perfected a clay target that was a flat disc instead of a ball. Ligowsky's first birds were made from clay that when baked, became almost indestructible. The birds flew well, but the baking was a problem. If the birds weren't hard enough, they crumbled during transportation. If they were hard enough to minimize damage in shipment, the shooters couldn't break them. More than one of Ligowsky's birds was knocked completely off its path without shattering. The characteristic bell-like sound they emitted under these circumstances was pleasing to the ear, but did little for the score.

Even with these drawbacks, the Ligowsky's clay pigeons won immediate approval from trapshooters in America as well as in England. Ligowsky's invention

brought trapshooting closer to the elimination of live
birds than even Portlock's glass balls. The first public
exhibition of the new target took place at the end of the
New York State Championship trapshoot at Coney Island
in 1880. This was the largest live-bird tournament ever
held up to that date, but the exhibition of the clay fac-
simile foreshadowed the end of the live-bird shooting.

A year after he introduced the clay target,
Ligowsky produced his own trap for throwing the discs.
With it, he established the first genuine degree of standardization in the sport. To introduce the public to his
target, Ligowsky hired the two best trap shooters in the
nation at that time to travel throughout the country, competing against each other using his clay pigeons. Capt.
A. H. Bogardus joined the famed W. F. "Doc" Carver
and together they toured the nation's trapshoots. The
tour was a great success, and sales soared.

Needless to say, other inventors jumped on the
band wagon, and many various forms of the disc and
trap were patented and sold. However, it remained for
an Englishman named McCaskey to add the final ingre-
dient that makes the game what it is today. Ligowsky's
clay bird was so durable that the hitting of the target
was too often in doubt. What the game needed was a bird
that would surely break when hit by only a few shot
pellets, but would also be strong enough to stand up to
handling, and finally being thrown from the trap.
McCaskey approached the problem as one of composition
rather than baking. Instead of clay he first used river
silt, held together by pitch. Eventually limestone was
substituted for river silt, and this bird made the grade.

Even though today's clay birds have no clay in them, Ligowsky's name has stuck to them. McCaskey's fully developed birds were sold as "Blue Rock" targets and the brand is still on the market today. Like Ligowsky,

The Ligowsky clay pigeon and trap, which really made possible the modern game.

McCaskey also developed a trap for his targets and marketed it under the name "Expert." It, too, is sold today and both trap and target, though they have undergone some modification, have changed very little in principle.

With uniform, practical targets and traps at last, trapshooting never looked back. Standardized conditions made competition possible between groups of shooters and clubs, and the growth of such shoots was rapid after the 1890's. Now the principal need was to formalize the game, with sets of rules that could provide a basis for rating a shooter's ability, no matter where he shot.

The first routine for shooting clay targets employed five traps set in a straight line; one man was up, the firing trap was a mystery and all the angles unknown. The shooter stood opposite the center trap (No. 3) and fired five shots. He had no idea from which of the five traps the target would come until after he called pull. Only the last target was certain.

Later, the reverse pull was introduced, in order to make the competition more difficult. In this game, five men were up at a time, one behind each trap. The gunner at No. 1 peg would get the bird from Trap 5, and so forth, with the man on peg 3 shooting the trap in front of him. But even this form of play needed refinement, and so the "walk-around system" was introduced. Instead of five shooters in a squad, there were six. The sixth man stood behind the shooter on Peg No. 1, and when they all fired, No. 5 became the walk-around man who came to the extra position on the first station. Each man fired one shot from each station and then walked to the next. The walk-around man was the spare.

This system was used until about 1885 when W. G. Sargent of Joplin, Missouri, originated the Sargent System. This game used three traps instead of five. The traps were four feet apart and threw targets at unknown angles. A year or two later, the five-man game, with five shots at each station from one trap, came into vogue and has been the dominant form since the turn of the century.

Undoubtedly, the sport of trapshooting would have grown on its own, without the formation of a central governing body to establish rules and set tournaments. However, the maturation into the sport as we know it today would have taken considerably longer. Today's Amateur Trap Association and its early counterparts can be credited with spurring on the growth and competitive aspects of trapshooting. Since the end of the 19th century, the growth and history of the Association has also been the growth and history of trapshooting.

The Interstate Manufacturer's and Dealer's Association was the forebear of what was eventually to grow into the Amateur Trapshooting Association. It was formed in 1890, not as the idea of any one person at that time, but more from a spontaneous need of a body of trapshooters to regularize their sport. They had no idea that their association would eventually become the backbone for the trapshooting movement in the United States and Canada.

During the first year, the Association held several tournaments, often called with little notice. Somehow the word got out, and the shoots were well attended. Because of the haphazard way in which the events were scheduled, the group decided to hold at least one shoot a year that everyone knew about. It was called the Grand American Handicap, and because it was their one big shoot of the year, live birds were used.

The first Grand American Handicap was held at Dexter Park, Long Island, New York in 1892. It proved to be such a success that the Association held their next year's shoot at the same place as a national shoot. Because of strong manufacturer overtones, the Association in 1895 changed its name to The Interstate Association. The group's Grand American Handicap grew each year and soon became the World Series of trapshooting.

1900 was a turning point for trapshooting and the Association in more than one way. Live birds were shot at the Grand, but a new event was added, the Grand American Handicap with clay targets. This seemed to stimulate a series of "sensational" newspaper articles condemning live-bird shoots. The press stirred the country's citizenry as well as its legislators and several states promptly passed laws banning live-bird shoots. Eventually, the Association gave in and in 1902, the last live-bird shoot was held at the Grand.

Trapshooting continued its rapid growth during the first quarter of the 20th century and the Grand American grew larger and larger, but there were problems. During the early years the Grand American migrated around the country, and as it grew, the problem of facilities and accommodations for the small army of shooters started to become insurmountable. In addition, there was rivalry between the professional shooters and industry representatives among Association members and those who considered the organization an amateur association,

The ATA grounds at Vandalia, Ohio, as they appeared in 1926

and Canadian resentment of the word "Interstate." In 1922, a name change was adopted, and the Interstate gave way to the American Trapshooting Association. Its officers believed the name change would also encourage Canadian shooters to join. They were wrong. Accordingly, in 1923, the American Trapshooting Association agreed to dissolve and let the Amateur Trapshooting Association become the governing body. The Association also decided to establish a permanent headquarters at Vandalia, Ohio, and to develop there a site for the annual Grand American Handicap. The ATA has been the governing body of the sport and Vandalia the site of the Grand American ever since.

Today the Grand American in August is still the unchallenged high-spot of the trapshooter's year. This year (1970) over four thousand shooters competing on 53 fields burned up about two and a half million shotshells in pursuit of Ligowsky's sometimes elusive clay target. It looks like the game is here to stay.

2 *Trap Guns & Equipment*

I have always felt that choosing a trap gun is like choosing a wife—everyone should pick his own. The choice of the gun or guns you shoot trap with is just as personal, and to a trapshooter, almost as important. Sure, it's easy to discuss the objective factors involved—type of action, barrel length, stock dimensions—and this chapter and the next are devoted precisely to such considerations. But beyond this, there's that intangible quality of "feel" that simply defies objective analysis, and you'll probably spend a lot of time trying different guns before you run across the one that has exactly the right feel for you. When you do find it, don't *ever* turn it loose. Like a wife, if you pick the right one, take care of it and don't abuse it, it will give you years of happiness and serve you well.

In making your selection you won't have to worry about the bore-size or gauge. As a practical matter, a 12-gauge is the only gun ever used for trap. No larger gauge is sanctioned for official competition, and while there's no law against using a 16 or 20, there's no advantage in it—quite the contrary. Normal loads in the smaller gauges carry significantly fewer pellets than the 388 shot in the standard trap load of 1⅛ ounces of 7½'s and produce a thinner pattern, all else being equal, at any yardage. The game is tough enough as it is without handicapping yourself further.

Another choice that isn't too difficult to make concerns barrel length. Trap guns are long-barreled guns, the standard factory option usually offering only a choice between 30- and 32-inch barrels, and sometimes 34 in break-open actions. For my money, the 30-inchers are fine in any style of action. I shoot 30-inch barrels myself, and recommend them to everyone except those giants like Dan Orlich who feel more comfortable with extra-long tubes. Actually, a 30-inch barrel on an autoloader or pump gun is equivalent to a 32-inch barrel on a single-shot or twin-tube shotgun because of the longer receivers in the former. I've always switched from my 30-inch pump to my 30-inch side-by-side without any ill effects, however—I guess I just like that barrel length.

Trap-Gun Actions

When it comes to choosing the type of action for your trap gun, there's considerably more latitude, since trap guns are made in every action-style the manufacturers produce, from the single-shot, single-barrel, and the single-barrel pump actions and autoloaders to the double-barreled side-by-sides and over-and-unders. Normal 16-yard and handicap shooters need only one shell at a time, and the traditional gun for them used to be the classic single-shot trap gun. But while the balance of the single-shot is excellent and its functioning simple, limited production has kept costs relatively high—too high for the average trapshooter who has to go out and get another gun for doubles. Looking down the line at the average trap tournament today, you'd have to conclude that the classic old single-shot is gradually passing from the scene.

There's considerably wider use of double-barreled shotguns, since they, like the pumps and autoloaders, can be used for double as well as 16-yard and handicap trap. The trap double, whether side-by-side or over-and-under, should always be equipped with a single trigger, now that these have gotten to be reasonably foolproof. (There was a time, though, when single triggers not infrequently doubled, a point you ought to keep in mind when you look at older guns that have seen a lot of use.) Many shooters prefer the over-and-under because of its single sighting plane, but I've always used a Winchester 21 side-by-side, bored Full and Full, for doubles, because it handles so sweetly. The principal drawback to

The five basic trap-gun actions, all Winchesters: top, the side-by-side double, a beautiful "Grand American" Model 21; next, the single most popular trap gun, the slide-action Model 12; center, the autoloader, a Model 1400; next, the classic single-shot, a Model 101; and bottom, an over-and-under (Model 101).

double-barreled guns is again cost, for they entail a lot of hand fitting and finishing and thus are expensive to manufacture.

If you survey the guns shooters bring to a big tournament like the Grand American at Vandalia, you'll find that the most popular action is the pump or slide action, and in particular, the Winchester Model 12. I've used a Model 12 as my 16-yard and handicap gun right from the start of my career, and I agree with a lot of other shooters that somehow nothing else balances quite as well. High production costs led to the discontinuance of the Model 12 in 1963 (except as a costly custom item), but persistent popular demand forced its reinstatement a decade later. The price of a Model 12—even a good used one—will put quite a dent in your pocketbook, but that's its only drawback. It's still an awful lot of gun for the money.

The popularity of the slide-action gun traces partly to its handling qualities and partly to its dependability. The long receiver makes for a very pointable, forward balance, and the normal place to put your left hand from the functional point of view—toward the rear of the forearm—also happens to be the ideal place in terms of shooting form. In addition, functioning is very positive, with little chance of breakdowns or malfunctions, even with hand-loaded fodder. For all these reasons, the pump is a fine gun for the job.

Nonetheless, I suspect that the coming action in trapshooting is probably the autoloader. Mechanical improvements have much improved its reliability with respect to the second shell, and a simple nipple device has been added to the shell exit port which effectively knocks down the spent hulls before they wing the shooter on the next peg. With these defects corrected, the autoloader offers several outstanding advantages. Not only does it share with the pump and the over-and-under the single sighting plane, and the advantage of using the same gun for everything, it has a further virtue that they lack: lessened recoil. In autoloaders a portion of the gasses and recoil from ignition are used to activate the bolt, thus substantially reducing the felt recoil for the shooter. This is of prime importance to young shooters, women and lightweight or elderly shooters, but it's an advantage for everyone, for there are few shooters who don't get a little flinchy from the pounding the shoulder takes in a long shoot-off.

Choke

Choke is the amount of constriction built into the last few inches of the barrel in order to control the shape and spread of the shot after it leaves the muzzle. Most trap guns come from the factory equipped with barrels that have been tested and/or designated Full Choke. A normal full-choke barrel will place 70 percent or more of its charge of pellets within a 30-inch circle when fired from a distance of 40 yards, according to standards established by the Sporting Arms and Ammunition Manufacturer's Institute. Most manufacturers try to place their barrels into percentage groups that probably range 10 points from minimum to maximum. However, some full-choke barrels throw a pattern that is much tighter, especially with modern plastic shells, and in extreme cases patterns run as high as 85 percent. For many shooters, this is too tight. I personally prefer a barrel that throws 70 to 75 percent patterns, and think that most shooters who want to win tournaments should do the same. Many shooters are using over-choked guns, thinking it will help them powder targets. This is especially true of shooters using foreign-made guns at 16 yards. These guns have a tendency to shoot too tightly. In this case, a little less choke might be all the difference needed to add a target or two to your score.

Following this reasoning, some shooters have a gunsmith open up the choke on their gun to get Improved-Modified (65 percent) or even straight Modified (60 percent) patterns. I suppose this is all right if all their competition shooting will take place from 16 yards, but I wouldn't do it myself and I hesitate to recommend it to other shooters. In any case, if you think that this is a solution to one of your problems, be sure that the choke work is done by a qualified gunsmith. And when you make the move, ream out only enough choke to put you in the top half of the percentages for the next lower choke.

Before you decide to change your choke or buy a new barrel with a different choke, pattern your shotgun. Beginning shooters seldom, if ever, pattern their guns, and in this they are no worse than experienced shooters. Even a large number of competitive shooters fail to take the time and effort to determine exactly what the choke in their gun is doing. They rely completely on the choke stamped by the manufacturer on the barrel, which may or may not have some relationship to reality.

Take the time, and you may be surprised. It's simple. Tack up a sheet of paper at least three feet square, at a measured distance of 40 yards from you. Place a mark at the center as an aiming point. Then, after you've shot, draw a 30-inch circle around the heaviest concentration of pellet marks. Count the pellets inside the circle and divide by 388 (for 7½'s) or 460 (for 8's). Do this four or five times, and take the average. Patterning your gun takes a little time, but it's the only way to know exactly where you stand.

Sights

Trap guns normally come equipped with both middle and front beads. These beads don't function as they would on a rifle, where the rear sight is lined up exactly behind the front sight. On a trap gun, the middle bead should be lined up just *under* the front bead, since it functions primarily as a reference point to show that the gun is correctly mounted in the shoulder pocket. (The true rear sight is, of course, the shooter's eye.) Incorrect mounting is common after prolonged shooting or at the end of the day when fatigue is more likely to affect a shooter's ability.

The middle sight is a characteristic of trap guns. The front sight is usually a rather large round ball of ivory, bone, metal or plastic. This middle sight is usually a bit smaller than the front sight. I don't like either of the sights to be larger than ⅛ inch. They are primarily reference points, and when they get too big, there is a tendency by some shooters to use them for conscious aiming. The shotgun should be pointed, like a finger, not aimed like a rifle.

Ribs

Sighting a trap gun is done along a raised, ventilated rib that extends the entire length of the barrel. The rib is elevated for two reasons—first, to create a continuous line from the end of the receiver to the end of the barrel which assists mightily in preventing cross-firing, and secondly, to permit the heat waves that are created by prolonged shooting on warm days to radiate more quickly from the hot barrel. Heat waves along the top of the barrel can distort the shooter's view of the target, making pickup more difficult and thus slower.

In actual shooting, the entire sighting plane isn't used, or at least it shouldn't be apparent to the shooter that it is being used. When the front bead is sitting on top of the middle bead, the front third of the sighting plane is foreshortened and the rear part of the plane drops out of focus because of its nearness to the shooter's eye. This foreshortening is intentional and desirable, because it produces a built-in vertical lead on straightaway as well as quartering shots, allowing the shooter to see the target over the barrel even though the barrel is actually on the bird. Otherwise, he would be forced to cover up the target to break it, as is commonly done in many field shooting situations.

In some trap models, the raised rib starts on the receiver instead of in front of it. It is thus raised even further off the barrel and brought closer to the line of sight between the eye and the target, eliminating even more the danger of false pointing.

Recoil Pads

Recoil pads, whether of rubber, leather or a combination of both, are standard equipment on trap stocks. They function primarily to help reduce the recoil a shooter must absorb, but they also help in a second, important way, by preventing the butt from slipping on the shoulder. Without a pad, this would be likely to occur in swinging to catch hard quartering targets. Once the butt is mounted in the shoulder pocket, a non-slipping rubber surface is more likely to keep it there.

Some shooters use an adjustable pad which enables them to vary the drop of their guns at will. I don't believe in this kind of thing very much, even though the theory is all right. I'd rather advise you to get the very best gun fit you can, as discussed in the next chapter, and then stick to it. With an adjustable pad there's always the temptation, when you drop a bird or two, to blame it on the pad and start tinkering with it. What you ought to be doing is thinking about the next bird, and getting your mind on fundamentals, not worrying whether you've got the pad just right. So try to get your pad as right as you can get it, and then leave it alone.

Loads

The ammunition companies designate four different loads as trap loads, all of them carrying $1\frac{1}{8}$ ounces of shot in the normal 2¾-inch shell. There's a light load charged with 2¾ drams equivalent of powder which is available in either 7½'s or 8's, and also a heavier, 3-dram equivalent load, offered in the same two shot sizes. In my experience, the best general-purpose load is the 2¾ dram equivalent charge with Number 8 shot. This is plenty for normal conditions up to 22 yards; you'll break your targets just as well as you would with the heavier load, and you'll find the load much easier on you. If there's enough wind to notice, I'd switch over to the light load of 7½'s; on a downright gusty day and for all handicap shooting beyond 22 yards, the right medicine is the 3-dram equivalent load of 7½'s. The heavier pellets hold their pattern and velocity just a little better under these more demanding conditions. Some shooters make a big fuss about different brands of shotshell, and think they can detect a difference in their patterns. Frankly, I doubt that it makes much difference, but maybe that's because I've always stuck to one company's products and never found any reason to change. I'll let you guess which one.

Clothing

What feels and looks good to you is the main thing that counts when it comes to trapshooting clothing, but once you've settled on something, stay with it long enough to get used to it. (I've know trapshooters who shot in the same sweater for fifty years.) The main thing is that it shouldn't be heavy or binding, or heavily padded at the shoulder, as some sweaters and vests are. Remember that changing the amount of shoulder padding or the weight of your clothing can change your stock fit. Some shooters compensate for this by switching to a thinner recoil pad in winter, when they're wearing heavier clothing. I prefer to keep the gun the same, and use several layers of thin clothing in winter so that I can retain warmth without adding bulk. The nylon "shell" shirt, worn between layers, is a great way of adding warmth without bulk, and I've often slipped one on as the afternoon cooled off.

Shoes should be relatively sturdy for comfort, and have a rubber or composition ground-gripping sole for steadiness. I don't like gloves very much, especially on my trigger finger, and I think they often affect the shooter's timing. There's something of a trend toward wearing gloves today, and shooters whose palms sweat under tension find that they benefit from them. But I'd recommend that if you don't need them, don't use them.

Glasses

Shooting glasses aren't quite as essential for protection for trapshooters as they are for skeet shooters, for the chances of a piece of target hitting you are remote. However, every serious trapshooter should own at least two pairs of glasses to help him cope with changing light conditions, for they can very noticeably affect how well he sees the targets. On bright, sunny days you'll need normal green or gray sun glasses, not too dark, but at least dark enough to keep you from squinting. The lenses should, of course, be large enough to keep you from seeing the rims.

Then for overcast days and shooting late in the afternoon I'd switch either to clear or to yellow-tinted glasses. They can really pay off if you happen to get into a shoot-off late in the day, at six or seven o'clock. I personally prefer the perfectly clear, untinted lenses, because the yellow lenses seem to irritate my eyes. They have a definite light-gathering quality, however, and if you can use them, so much the better.

Ear Plugs

There are lots of good ear plugs on the market, from simple ones all the way up to fancy custom-fitted jobs, and I think every trapshooter ought to find a form he likes and use them. I prefer the in-the-ear plugs to the muff-type, but that's just a matter of taste. Ear plugs not only minimize the danger of hearing loss, but also help concentration by cutting down on background noise, at lease for most people. I've heard some shooters claim that ear plugs disrupted their shooting, and you can choose to do without them if you wish, but don't blame your hearing loss on me!

3 *Gun Fit*

How you break the bird—whether you break it—
depends on where the gun is pointing when you touch it
off, and how you tracked the target. But these depend, in
turn, on your shape, the gun's shape and how they fit
together once the gun has been mounted. It's essential that
your gun fit you correctly, for if it doesn't fit, much of the
time, effort and money you put into improving your
shooting will go right down the drain. (Of course, it's
just as essential for you to know how to mount the gun
correctly, for even a perfect gun fit can't help you if you

put the gun up wrong. This subject is important enough to rate a chapter all to itself, and it is treated separately in the next chapter. Here we are concerned with the subtleties of the fit of the gun alone.)

There are many shooters today who are shooting guns that do not fit them and are still breaking good scores. The real question is, however, how much better could they be if their guns were fitted correctly? It seems to me that shooting a ill-fitting gun is like wearing shoes that don't fit you. You can get where you're going, but it takes longer and it's less pleasant getting there.

Gun fit is important to the trapshooter because of the speed at which the game is played, on the one hand, and the length to which it is played—call it the fatigue factor—on the other. With targets thrown at unknown angles, the shooter must start swinging on them almost instantaneously in order to break them. The flight of the bird is so fast that no time can be spent in readjusting the gun once it's mounted; there is no time to wrap yourself around the gun and aim, as in rifle shooting, there is only time to look. The gun must point where you look—automatically—if you are to break targets consistently. If this congruence is a result of contortion on your part in order to adapt to a poorly fitting gun, you'll be able to break targets for a while, but as fatigue catches up with you in a long race, you'll drop targets you should have hit.

Factory Dimensions

Trap guns have standard dimensions as they come from the factory, and probably three shooters out of four

GUN MEASUREMENT

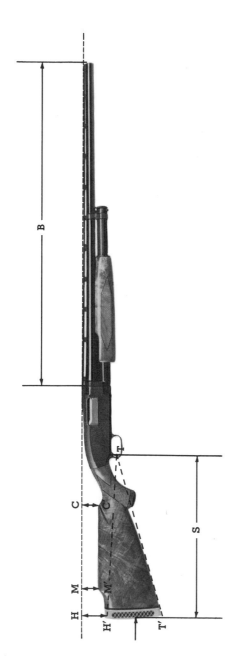

B = Length of barrel.
S = Length of stock (Pull).
HH' = Drop at heel of butt.
MM' = Drop at heel of monte.
CC' = Drop at comb.

TH' = Length stock at heel ⎫
TT' = Length stock at toe   ⎬ determine pitch.
                                          ⎭

can get by with the unaltered gun. Some lucky shooters are fitted perfectly by the standard dimensions (usually about 14⅜ inches length of pull, 1⅜ inches drop at comb and 1⅞ inches drop at heel) and many others will find these measurements close enough to enable them to shoot pretty well with them. But if you're serious about your shooting, you're going to want to have your gun fit *perfectly*, especially if you're the one shooter out of four who doesn't get by too well with the factory stock. This means finding out what your right measurements are, and altering the stock to match them.

The factory dimension that causes the most problems is the length of pull, for 14⅜ inches is too long, in my judgment, for the majority of shooters. Of course, it's the only practical thing for the factory to do, because you can always cut some stock off while you can't very well stretch one. In practice, however, you can shoot better with a gun that's too short than one that's too long. This is due to the fact that on quartering or hard-angle shots, the long stock will bind and kill your swing, and your head will tend to come off the gun. Too short a stock will permit you to bust targets, but you'll find yourself busting your own nose as well with your right thumb.

The correct length of stock is one that finds your cheek located half an inch to an inch in back of the base of your right thumb when you have mounted the gun correctly. The old "guesstimate" way of checking stock length, by measuring it against the inside of your forearm, isn't foolproof, but it's often pretty close. If you have to really stock-crawl to put your cheek that far forward, the stock is too long for you, while if your nose

Placing the butt in the crook of your elbow, as shown above, is the easiest way to judge if the stock length is approximately correct. It's not infallible, but it's usually pretty close.

is pushed right up against your thumb, the stock is too short.

Drop

Drop at comb is the single most critical stock dimension, for comb height determines the elevation of your eye in relation to the bore, and, of course, in shotgun shooting your eye is really the rear sight. Drop at heel is more a matter of comfort, since it determines where the buttstock will rest against your shoulder, once you've cheeked the stock.

If you know how to mount a gun correctly (and if you don't, you'll learn how in the next chapter), there's a pretty good self-test you can make to check up on drop. You simply shut your eyes, mount the gun and ease your head forward and down onto the comb, holding it there with slight pressure. When you open your eyes, you should be looking straight down the rib, and you should see the front bead sitting right on top of the middle bead. If you can't see the front bead at all, the stock has too much drop; if you see some rib between the two beads, the stock is too straight for you. It's as simple as that. But take your time before you whittle away at comb height. In trap you're shooting at a rising target, and you want a slightly high-shooting gun, and hence, a stock that's on the straight side —for you.

The Monte Carlo Stock

While the standard straight trap stock is preferable for the bulk of shooters, individuals with long necks and sloping shoulders find it too uncomfortable for them.

If they seat the butt-stock properly in the shoulder pocket, they've got to "stock crawl" to place their cheek against the comb, while if they really bring the gun up to their face, the heel of the butt rises up over the top of the shoulder. The Monte Carlo stock is the answer to such problems. This is a special-purpose trap stock in which the drop at comb is carried all the way back in a straight line, dropping down to the "drop at heel" dimension only an inch or so short of the butt itself (see diagram). Many normally proportioned shooters also prefer the Monte Carlo stock configuration, on the principle that no matter where your cheek hits the comb, the gun fit will be the same. This is true, but it doesn't stop a lot of shooters who use conventional stocks from going straight. I think I shoot a little better with the Monte Carlo myself, but I don't insist on it for others.

Pitch

Pitch is the measurement, in inches at the muzzle, of the sighting plane's deviation from a true vertical when the buttstock is squarely placed against a 90-degree horizontal. (The practical way to measure pitch is against a doorjamb, with the butt squarely on the sill.) Pitch depends partly on barrel length, and long-barreled, high-shooting guns like trap guns require relatively little pitch. An inch is fairly standard, in a 30-inch trap gun, and some shooters prefer no pitch at all. (Skeet guns and field guns commonly show a couple of inches of pitch.)

If you seat the butt squarely in your shoulder pocket, changing the pitch of your stock by removing wood from the toe or heel (or by using shims) will change

90° pitch

SHOTGUN PITCH

the point of impact, and also, of course, the sight picture. I prefer to keep the sight picture constant, with the top bead sitting directly on top of the middle bead. In these circumstances changes in pitch and will affect comfort only, and depend primarily on the conformation of your shoulder. Thick-shouldered or heavy-chested shooters need more down-pitch to keep the toe of the stock from digging into their shoulder.

Cast-off

A rather subtle adjustment in gun fitting in which the British place great store is cast-off, or cast-on, as the case may be. This is the lateral deviation of the butt from the line of sight, and though most foreign guns have a certain amount of cast-off cut into them (though rarely as much as half an inch), most American-stocked guns have no cast at all. Cast-off is supposed to enable you to face your targets more squarely, and minimize any need to incline your head laterally. I wouldn't say it doesn't, but it's not an adjustment for which I've ever found any particular need, and I've fitted an awful lot of shooters.

Trigger Weight

Technically, the weight of a shotgun's trigger pull is also part of gun fitting, since personal preferences vary and good shoooters can be found who prefer pulls as different as two pounds and ten pounds, I suppose it should be considered another variable. Personally, I don't think a trap gun's trigger pull should ever be less than three pounds or more than about five, with four to four and a half pounds the ideal. Too fine a trigger pull—below three pounds—requires so little exertion to fire the gun that it can lead to premature firings. This is especially true when the shooter is swinging after a target quartering hard either to the right or to the left. His tendency is to pull the trigger with the swing of the gun as he goes after the bird, and he often fires before he has actually caught the bird.

Getting Fitted

How does the less experienced trap shooter find out how well his gun fits him? Probably the safest way is to get yourself checked out by a top professional coach or to seek the advice of a professional shooter representing one of the several trap gun manufacturers. These people are in the business and are trained to help shooters with such problems. They also probably have access to a "try gun," a shotgun whose stock is adjustable in all key dimensions. The "pro" can alter the try gun until it fits you, and then read off the dimensions so that you can have a stock altered to match them.

Gun shops also sometimes have personnel capable

Trigger weight is determined
by using a scale hooked to
the trigger. The ideal pull is
between three and five pounds.

A try-gun in the hands of
an expert fitter is a fine way
to determine correct individual
stock dimensions. The stock of
the try-gun is adjustable
for drop at both comb and heel,
length of pull, pitch and cast-off.

of fitting the gun to you, and the top-notch ones even sometimes have try guns. But be cautious; some gun shop personnel are salesmen who rarely shoot at all, much less shoot trap, and life being what it is, they're in the business of making a sale with the least amount of inconvenience. More often than not, they'll try to get you to settle for what they've got, which is factory dimensions. Now, don't get me wrong—factory dimensions are in fact a pretty good average of what a lot of shooters can use, but until they start pouring all mankind out of the same mold, it's obvious that no one set of dimensions is going to be equally satisfactory to everybody.

Perhaps the surest way of finding exactly what dimensions fit you is also the longest way, but also the one most of our top trapshooters have used—by experimenting and "looking around." Phil Miller once told me that "Every man is entitled to one great bird dog and one good trap gun in a life time. All you have to do is keep looking until you find them." I have come to believe him! Let me just add this: Once you find the *right* gun, put the bill of sale in your wife's name and lock it in the safe deposit box so that you cannot sell or trade it!

There are few places where trapshooters congregate, whether at tournaments, clubhouses or gun shops, where there aren't a few trap guns for sale or trade. Pick up one that looks good to you, open the action—something you should do with *every* gun, *every* time you pick it up—and then put it up to your shoulder. As your gun-mounting becomes grooved, you'll become aware of marked differences in the way different guns come up, and occasionally one will give you an "I-can-score-with-this-gun" feeling. When you find one that produces scores to match the feeling, hang onto it, if possible; if not, make a note of its stock dimensions and compare them to those of your own gun. Remember, nobody ever said this was the quickest or the cheapest way; but then, for a lot of shooters, hunting for the perfect gun is also fun, and you can't stop them anyway

4 *Gun Mounting & Basic Stance*

Once in shooting position, the shooter has four points of physical contact with his gun—left hand, right hand, cheek and shoulder. Gun mounting is concerned with how these contacts are established. It consists, in brief, of grasping the shotgun between both hands, pushing it forward and lifting it almost horizontally, pulling it back until it makes contact with the cheek, and then bedding it snugly against the shoulder. It all sounds pretty simple, and in the end it is. There are right and wrong ways of accomplishing each step, however, and even the smallest details make a difference. Many shooters never succeed in mastering all the elements of correct gun mounting. Let's take a look at each of them, one by one, and then consider some of the reasoning behind them.

Let's start with the position of the hands. The left hand should be positioned relatively far back on the forearm, on the back third, in the case of most slide actions or autoloaders, the fingers lightly supporting the fore-end from underneath, the thumb extended forward. This "short" left arm position is one of the important keys to successful trapshooting, especially when combined with a light grip and a relatively high position of the elbow. The short hold provides leverage for following sharply rising targets, and enables the shooter to swing the gun through a greater arc after quartering targets as well. The elevated left elbow balances the similarly placed right elbow, and facilitates a smooth and accurate lateral swing.

The right hand grasps the pistol grip of the stock slightly from underneath, in such a way that the trigger finger will have a relatively straight pull instead of a sharply downward one, with the thumb opposing the fingers. The index finger should contact the trigger precisely in the crease of the first joint, counting from the fingernail. The right elbow, like the left, is elevated as high as it will go without forcing.

The elevation of the right elbow is particularly important, for it is this detail that really creates the shoulder pocket for the butt. Holding the gun too far out on the shoulder, or even on the biceps, is the commonest fault in gun mounting. When the right elbow is correctly

The end result of the gun-mounting
routine. Note especially the "short" left
arm, the hand gripping the rear portion of
the fore-end. This is a prime key to a
smooth swing.

Proper gun mounting, seen from the front.
The high position of both elbows is the
main point to notice here. This is a hard
virtue to exaggerate, and most shooters
have the opposite problem.

elevated, the shoulder pocket will be seen to be quite a
specific place, a slightly concave area just below the collar bone where it joins the round, knobby upper joint of
the humerus. The buttstock should rest on the large pec-
toral muscle rather than on the collarbone itself, and the
heel of the butt should not project above the shoulder,
though it should not fall more than half an inch or so
below it.

The contact with the trigger by the first joint of
the finger instead of the fleshy tip is also a small detail
of considerable importance. The fleshy pad on the finger-

Wrong trigger
contact. The index
finger should not be
hooked around the
trigger in such a way
that the fleshy seg-
ment between the
first two joints is used
to pull the trigger.
The pull will have
too much give, and
timing will be
uncertain.

Contact still wrong. If only the fleshy pad at the tip of the index finger is used, the same problem will exist: uncertain timing.

Correct trigger contact. Contact should be with the crease of the first joint from the fingertip. There is no padding here, and timing will always be the same.

tip has enough "give" to throw your timing off if you fail to allow for it perfectly. The crease of the first joint has none, and is always the same.

In mounting, you first place the gun in a ready position, horizontal with the ground and with the stock just above hip level. Next, smoothly push it forward until it clears the body and lift it, still keeping it horizontal, until the comb makes contact with your cheek; then draw the buttstock back toward your shoulder, which should push forward slightly to meet it, and as the buttstock settles against your shoulder, let your head sink gently down and forward to produce a moderate but perceptible pressure between cheek and comb.

It is important to practice mounting the gun until you can be sure of seating the butt correctly in the shoulder pocket every time you put it up. With the butt firmly in the shoulder pocket, the shooter needn't lean his face sideways over the stock—only a slight forward, downward movement of the face will place it exactly at the same place on the stock. With the stock placed properly in the pocket, the stock will in fact come up to the cheek, and only a slight pressure by the cheek will be required to establish the correct sight picture.

Work on your gun mounting until you can do it correctly almost in your sleep. The essence of gun fit and gun mounting is putting the gun in exactly the same relation to the shooter's eye every time, with no need for subsequent adjustment. Only when this has been achieved is the shooter free to concentrate on picking up his target at its unknown angle, and that's plenty.

The Shooter's Stance

A shooter's address at the firing line can be broken down into two elements, *position* and *stance*. By position, I mean how and where the shooter places his feet in relation to the traphouse. By stance, I mean the attitude of his body after he has planted his feet and assumed his position. If his position is correct, the shooter's stance is somewhat less crucial. Nonetheless, it materially affects his shooting comfort, and thus involves stamina, consistency and ultimately winning and losing.

Stance and style vary considerably, even among good shooters, and I can't deny that I've seen some marvelous scores shot from some pretty strange-looking stances. But why do it the hard way?

Correct address position: easy and natural-looking, relatively erect, yet solid and stable.

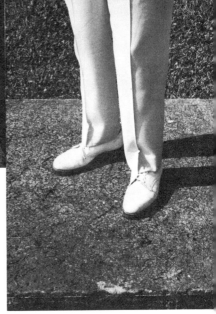

Two views of the correct foot position. The toes are splayed slightly outward for added stability, but the base is relatively narrow in order to avoid impeding rotational swing. Toes are not much more than a foot apart, heels somewhat less.

To establish a correct stance, the shooter faces the traphouse, his left foot slightly forward, his right foot 8 to 10 inches to the side, with the toes of both feet spread slightly outward. An imaginary line drawn across his toes should describe an angle of about 45 degrees from the traphouse. He then mounts the gun as described above. This position, with the left foot advanced and the toes slightly splayed, is a highly stable one. The splayed feet provide good lateral stability, while the slightly advanced left foot contributes stability from front to rear.

Front-to-rear stability is particularly important, of course, because of the fact that recoil will push the shooter backward as soon as the shot is fired. He must anticipate and compensate for this by leaning slightly forward in the direction of the traphouse. This slight forward lean is accomplished by slightly "cracking" the left knee.

The correct address viewed from the side.
The left knee need be bent only slightly,
and the right leg should remain fully
extended.

As the left knee is bent, the back leg extends almost rigidly to retain contact with the ground. The bent front leg then serves as the pivot in swinging, while the back leg becomes the anchor point. Even in pivoting to swing with a sharply quartering target, however, the left leg is only slightly altered; this is because most of the swinging motion should take place above the waist. Tracking the target with the gun should be accomplished primarily with the left hand. As it nears its limit of mobility, additional swing is contributed by the shoulders, and for the maximum arc, twisting at the waist comes into play. *The feet stay planted.*

Bending the left knee will, of course, shift a certain amount of weight forward, and this is desirable as long as the shooter still feels that he is balanced pretty evenly on the balls of both feet. For generally, near-even weight distribution between both feet is a characteristic of most of the better trapshooters, unlike the situation in skeet. The trapshooter has only a relatively short arc to swing through compared to the skeet shooter, since all of his targets are outgoers. He needs stability and comfort more than maximum flexibility, and an even balance on both feet tends to mean less fatigue, thus enabling him to remain at his best for a longer period of time.

If you find yourself running out of gun swing too early, the chances are that your weight is too far back, your stance is too wide or that you're poorly positioned in relation to the traphouse for the particular station you're shooting from. In general, of course, you should be facing the area in which you expect to break your tar-

A common shooting stance, but wrong. Too wide a
base, too much forward lean, too low a right elbow.
The whole position lacks ease and naturalness, and
the shooter using it will tire in a long race.

gets. This is simple in the case of skeet—you even have
a stake to mark the crossing point as a reference. In trap
you have unknown angles to contend with, but you do
know, within certain limits, where the birds *won't* go.

The exact details of positioning are discussed,
station by station, in Chapter 6. The principle involved
is that you position yourself at each station with primary
reference to the straightaway target, but that you "favor"
the most difficult angle you anticipate from that post.

Knowing that right-handed shooters swing more easily to the left than to the right, for example, the Station 5 position is slightly to the right of the normal position for the straightaway target, favoring the tough right-angling bird by putting you in a position from which you won't have to swing so far for it.

When in doubt about stance, remember that it

Another incorrect stance. This shooter thinks his weight is forward because he's bending over so far, but actually his weight is back in his tail. In addition, the left hand is too far forward. You can still break targets this way, but it's much harder to develop a smooth swing and consistent scores.

should be stable, natural and comfortable. It will be, if you have followed the method for building your stance that we have described above. It's not the only way, and you'll see some fine scores shot from a whole range of exaggerated stances. You can even categorize shooters as to crouchers, squatters, leaners and so on. These shooters may think that their success depends on their style, but in reality they're just making it harder for themselves. Leave the extreme, exaggerated stances to them; learn the correct stance yourself, and stick to it. It's a whole lot more comfortable, and in the long run you'll score better because of it.

5 *Pick-up, Leads & Timing*

Picking up the target soon after it leaves the trap and breaking it quickly are two prime attributes of the skillful trapshooter. Just where you break the target during its flight is very important, and easily stated: the closer, the better. Good timing will not only enable you to break more singles targets from 16 yards, but even more important, it will give you a sound foundation for shooting handicap targets and doubles trap later on.

Some shooters have a natural ability to pick up a target with uncanny speed after it leaves the traphouse.

Others must allow the target to move along a fair part of its flight before they can distinguish the bird and have it register in their minds. At the beginning of its flight, the bird is moving at about 80 feet per second, a speed that the human eye registers only as a blur. No shooter, no matter how fast his reflexes, should try to shoot at the target while it's in this blurred state.

Most shooters don't have this problem, but incline toward the opposite one, waiting too long to pull the trigger. *Always break the target as soon as you can see it distinctly and mark its course.* As soon as you react, swing onto the target, take the proper lead, and pull the trigger. The longer you hesitate, the farther out the bird will travel, and the greater will be the chances for errors and a miss. As soon as you're on the target, break it. Never hesitate or "ride out" the bird. Riding out targets is one of the worst habits in trapshooting. If you want to improve your score, you've got to kick this habit as soon as possible.

Picking up a target quickly isn't difficult if you know the right method and have no bad habits to break; inexperienced shooters often acquire the right technique quite readily. The key to it is this: After you've mounted the gun, just before you call for the bird, transfer your vision out beyond the traphouse and *look for the bird.* Keep the muzzle of your gun in your peripheral vision, but focus your eyes on infinity, not on the end of your barrel or on the traphouse. Call for the bird, and look for it; as soon as it appears, focus on it, swing your gun and establish your lead, and fire. The bird should break within 20 yards of the trap if you did it right.

Some shooters fall back on the excuse that their pattern hasn't fully opened at close yardages. This just isn't that true. The amount of pattern spread you gain between 26 and 36 yards is less than a foot. In reality, these shooters usually haven't persuaded themselves to shoot at the closer ranges. In fact, most shooters actually do pick up the bird quickly enough, but they wait on it, riding it out, until it arrives at the spot where they feel "sure" of a hit. They don't realize that there are no second chances for corrections or alterations in pointing once the bird approaches the apex of its flight. Too often, the bird ends up lost.

Some shooters rationalize that breaking the bird is all that counts, no matter how, where or with what style. This type of reasoning holds back some potentially good shooters who could easily improve if they'd ever convince themselves to take the bird as soon as they are on it. Riding it out will also create the tendency to stop the swing and result in underleading the target. Unfortunately, it is sometimes difficult for experienced shooters to break this habit, for they get set in their ways. If you try to coach them out of the habit, they'll go along with you for a while. But after they miss three or four birds, they want to go back to the old ways. What they forget is that they are trying to improve. And trying to improve often means using a different approach.

Eye Dominance

Not infrequently the real villain, with shooters who ride out their targets, is insufficient eye dominance, for eye dominance has considerable influence on the shooter's performance, and especially on pick-up. It works like this: The right-handed shooter whose right eye is dominant can shoot with both eyes open. He has a wider range of peripheral vision and better depth perception than the one-eyed shooter, and can hold a higher gun and still pick up the target easily. The shooter with cross-dominance or no established dominance must shoot with one eye closed or blocked, and must hold on top of the traphouse in order to be sure of seeing the bird promptly. He can still become a champion—many one-eyed shooters have—but he'll have to work harder at it.

A surprising number of shooters aren't even aware of eye dominance, yet one eye is normally dominant over the other when picking up an object and pointing it out. Usually, eye dominance corresponds to body dominance—a right-handed person normally has a dominant right eye and the left-handed person, a dominant left eye. Occasionally the dominance will shift back and forth, with no established dominance existing. In extreme cases, there is cross-dominance—the left eye dominating in a right-handed person, interfering with his ability to aim and point a gun mounted to his right shoulder whenever he leaves both eyes open.

The commonest problem is insufficient dominance. In order to shoot properly, such shooters must squint, close or block out their left eye in order to insure dominance of the right eye. Some shooters who have this problem may not realize it, and attribute their misses to other causes. Determining eye dominance is a simple trick. An easy way is to take a clay target and knock the

An easy way to test your eye dominance, using a target
with the center knocked out. First, close your left eye and
frame some object with the target, like this palm tree. Next,
open your left eye. If the object stays in the hole with
both eyes open, your right eye is dominant. However, if
the object seems to move out of the hole when you open
your left eye and appears instead to the left of it, then your
left eye is dominant. Check this by closing your right eye
when aiming at the palm tree; if you are left-eyed, the
tree will stay in place.

hole out of its center. Hold it in your right hand, extend it to arm's length and close the left eye. With your right eye, center the hole on an object in the distance. Then open your left eye. If the hole jumps to the right of the object, your left eye is the master eye. If on the other hand the object stays inside the hole, then your right eye is the master eye

If the hole and object keep shifting back and forth, you'll have to try to train your right eye to hold onto the object while keeping the left open. If you can't do this, it's best to solve the problem mechanically, either by squinting your left eye closed, putting a shade over it or getting glasses with a dot on the left lens. In any case, this problem cannot be treated lightly.

Leads

Once a clay target has left the traphouse, its flight, for all but straightaways, is a composite of two directions —vertical and horizontal, rising and quartering. (Of course, rising also implies falling, but since the trap-shooter always attempts to break his targets on the rise, the falling phase should be academic.) *All* birds rise, but not all birds quarter. The amount of rise may seem large to the shooter observing it over the rib of a gun, but in reality the rise left in a target 16 yards from the trap under normal wind conditions is relatively small. However, because of this constant characteristic of trap-target flight, trap guns normally have a certain amount of vertical lead built into them, by means of their straight stock dimensions and limited pitch.

ARC OF TARGET FLIGHT
SHOWING ELEVATIONS

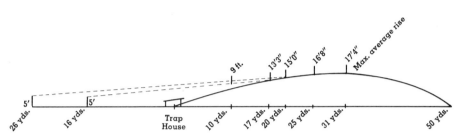

The normal arc of a trap target's flight. In singles, targets are broken about 20 yards from the traphouse, or about 36 yards from the shooter. But even in doubles, the second target should be broken before it starts to fall, in other words, within 30 yards of the traphouse.

Vertical Lead

As a practical matter, the amount of vertical lead built into the trap gun is usually sufficient, except for long handicap yardages, to compensate for the bird's rising flight.

This is apparent when you analyze the flight of a bird and study the figures. A regulation trap is designed to throw the target a distance of 50 yards from the house. The machine doesn't throw every bird the same height above the ground, but a regulation target must be thrown so that at a point 10 yards in front of the house, the target rise will be between 6 and 12 feet.

In practice, the average flight of a bird has been

calculated to rise 9 feet above the ground at a point 10 yards from the house. However, most shooters do not get onto the bird, ready to fire, until it has already traveled some 20 yards from the trap. At this point the target is 6 feet higher, or 15 feet above the ground. Eleven yards later, the target has reached the apex of its average flight, 17 feet, 4 inches above the ground. The target should always be shot before it begins to descend. Once its downward direction begins, it loses speed and the flight path becomes less predictable.

If a shooter picks up the target at 20 yards and fires immediately, the bird can rise only 2 feet, 4 inches before it starts to fall. The 32-inch spread of a full-choke shotgun pattern at 36 yards (20 yards from the trap, plus the 16 yards the shooter is behind the trap) will more than allow for any missing vertical lead. Thus, there's no vertical lead that isn't covered by the high-shooting qualities of the gun and the spread of the shot.

Horizontal Lead

Horizontal or lateral lead is something else again. The mathematical lead required on each target is fixed and calculable, and one might think that once a shooter knew these figures he could break every target. However, the actual lead is often quite different from the apparent lead—apparent to the shooter, that is. The apparent lead must reckon in a shooter's reaction time and muscular coordination. One shooter may need a 3-foot apparent lead to break a target, while another shooter with faster reflexes may accomplish it with only an ap-

TABLE OF COMPUTED LEADS

Station	Target Position	16 Yds. Hor. Lead (In.)	16 Yds. Vert. Lead (In.)	20 Yds. Hor. Lead (In.)	20 Yds. Vert. Lead (In.)	26 Yds. Hor. Lead (In.)	26 Yds. Vert. Lead (In.)
1	1	0	7	0	9	0	14
	2	10	7	12	9	17	14
	3	19	8	24	10	33	15
	4	27	10	35	12	47	16
	5	35	12	44	14	60	18
2	1	10	7	12	9	17	14
	2	0	7	0	9	0	14
	3	10	7	12	9	17	14
	4	19	8	24	10	33	15
	5	27	10	35	12	47	16
3	1	19	8	24	10	33	15
	2	10	7	12	9	17	14
	3	0	7	0	9	0	14
	4	10	7	12	9	17	14
	5	19	8	24	10	33	15
4	1	27	10	35	12	47	16
	2	19	8	24	10	33	15
	3	10	7	12	9	17	14
	4	0	7	0	9	0	14
	5	10	7	12	9	17	14
5	1	35	12	44	14	60	18
	2	27	10	35	12	47	16
	3	19	8	24	10	33	15
	4	10	7	12	9	17	14
	5	0	7	0	9	0	14

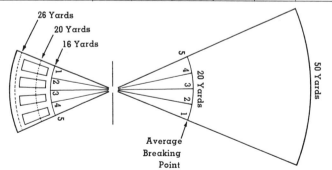

26 Yards
20 Yards
16 Yards

50 Yards

20 Yards

Average Breaking Point

adapted from the NRA Shotgun Handbook.

parent 1-foot lead. It becomes obvious, then, that tables of computed actual leads are valuable primarily to show the relationship between different target paths, and cannot be depended upon as valid working distances for every shooter.

The easiest way to use these figures is by translating them into barrel widths. It works this way: The barrel of a 12-gauge gun is 1 inch wide. Held to the shoulder and sighted over, this 1-inch barrel covers a 12-inch area at 36 yards (the distance at which most 16-yard shooters will break their targets). A 2-foot lead then becomes two barrel widths from the 16-yard line.

A 3-inch lead at the muzzle is what the average shooter needs on the most sharply quartering birds. Top shooters may not use that much lead—the average is nearer a 1-foot actual jump on the target—but shooters with slower reactions usually need a longer lead. And a foot or two of excess, at the target, will still permit the bird to be broken. It is almost impossible to overlead a target, horizontally, while it's very easy to underlead it.

The reason lies in the shot string. Those shooters who do overlead benefit from the way shot pellets leave the barrel. The shot does not leave the muzzle like a flat pancake of lead, without depth. At 36 yards, the "string" of shot is more cone-shaped, about 3 feet in diameter and about 12 feet long. Some of the shot at the head of the column will reach the crossing path of the target too early and pass without striking. But somewhere in the 12-foot column, the path of shot and target will cross. After the pellets hit the target, there is likely to be a lot of lead still behind. The 12-foot string then becomes a

12-foot contact area that breaks targets even though the shooter may have been so far ahead that only the shot at the tail of the column was used to break the target.

That's why it's so easy to underlead a quartering target. If the end of the barrel never reaches or passes the target, because of reaction time, shot-travel times, as well as improper pointing, the shot never has a chance to get near the target. This is the primary form of under-leading.

Follow-through

The average shooter frequently suffers another form of underleading, which derives from stopping the gun. These shooters insist that they *do* lead the bird, that they even take very long leads, but still miss. They attribute this to overleading. In reality, the opposite is true. Their misses are behind the bird because they stop the swing. The sequence goes something like this. The shooter catches the bird, passes it and thinks immediately that the lead is too much. He stops for a fraction of time to let the bird catch up and then shoots. It takes the average shooter sixty-five hundredths of a second to get a shot off after he decides it's time to shoot. In that time, the target has traveled about 4 feet.

Although he may have been the right distance ahead of the bird when he was swinging, he is now two or more feet behind the target. There is no way that the bird and the shot will ever meet. In his mind, the shooter honestly believes that he was ahead of the bird. He missed, so he is sure that he overled the target. In reality, he stopped still and was behind the bird when he fired.

This builds a case for follow-through in trap, even though the horizontal swing trapshooting requires is minimal when compared to skeet. But if you don't need much follow-through on vertical targets, you're lost without it on lateral swings. You'll start stopping too soon and finish by shooting behind the bird.

Most shooters do try to follow-through with their guns and appreciate that what happens after you pull the trigger is influenced by what happened before you decided to fire. But there's another kind of follow-through that is equally important, and it too can affect what happens after you pull the trigger. It's following through with your attention as well as your gun. If you want to improve your scores, you must get in the habit of following through with your eyes and head, of continuing to watch both your barrel and the target, even as it breaks and falls to the ground.

Too many shooters, beginners and experienced shots alike, have a tendency to pull the trigger and then jerk their heads up to see if they hit the target. You should be able to see if you hit the target even with your head on the gun, if you have been leading properly. Your head and eye must stay lined with the end of the barrel *until the target falls*. Otherwise, your tendency to look up will grow with every shot. This action will move closer and closer to the moment you pull the trigger and can lead to your lifting your eyes and head even before the shot is fired. Proper head and eye follow-through is just as important as following through with the swing of the gun.

There's a truism in trapshooting that shooters

"fear the angles but miss the straightaways." Shooters often dread hard angling shots and think they miss them because of incorrect leads, but an examination of their scores often shows that they miss more straightaways than angles. The reason is that on left-angling shots, the shooter is pushing the stock into his face, preserving the relationship between his line of vision and the gun, while on right-angling shots he learns to push his face into the stock. On straightaways, however, there is nothing to help him keep his face on the stock, and it can come off all too easily. In fact, on straightaways you don't even have to lift your head off the gun to miss; just raising your eyes can be enough.

This characteristic, combined with the tendency of many shooters to hold too long on a straightaway, make it the most deceiving bird in the game. Often when the bird comes out of the traphouse the shooter is concentrating so hard on picking it up that he forgets to keep his gun pointing where he's looking. In looking for the bird some shooters raise their eyes, some their whole head. This lifts the line of sight and so elevates the gun. As a result, the shot is over the bird, and misses. Keep your head down when you look for the bird and your eyes on the shooting plane, and you won't have this trouble with straightaway birds.

Similar to the problems of straightaways are birds with very slight angles, birds which quarter only slightly. Many shooters misinterpret these gentle angles as straightaways and shoot to the center side of the target. Occasionally, they are lucky and catch these targets with the edge of their pattern, but more often, they miss. The answer is to read the target correctly and hold it in with your pattern, by pointing outside it.

Angles are basically easier to shoot because they are easier to pick up after they leave the traphouse. With the straightaway, the apparent movement of the target is just a few feet, while in angling shots the apparent movement is much greater. This greater apparent movement makes it easier to see the target, while the angle also gives the shooter more time to get ready and to shoot. A third characteristic that makes quartering shots easier is the shot-string effect. There is only the pattern spread on straightaways, while on angling shots you have the pattern spread as well as the string working for you.

Position & Hold: A Five-Station Analysis

6

An essential fact of life for the trapshooter is that while he never knows in advance the angle at which the next bird will be thrown, he *does* know some angles at which it *can't* be thrown, at least legally. Or perhaps I should say that he *ought* to know these illegal angles, for the surprising thing, in a game so strong in built-in unknowns, is the fact that many shooters never take the time to study and analyze the field itself, and only know that the shooting stations fall on an arc starting 16 yards behind the center of the traphouse. Needless to say, their ignorance costs them targets.

In the discussion of the shooter's basic stance in Chapter 4, I stated that the positioning of the shooter in relationship to the traphouse—the particular placement of his feet, in effect—was even more crucial to his score than the basic attitude of his body, important as that was. The reason why, of course, is that foot position determines how easily the shooter will be able to swing through the arc of possible target angles. Accordingly, any discussion of the shooter's positioning on the trapfield must start with an understanding of the trapfield itself.

The shape and area of the field over which targets fly is actually a mirror image of the field the shooters occupy behind the traphouse. The maximum angle between Stations 1 and 5 is also the maximum angle of variation from one side of the trapfield to the other. A 16-yard trap is capable of throwing its target in more than 70 different directions within this arc, and thus the gunner has no idea where the target will go until it is in flight. However, any trapshooter can be pretty sure where a target *won't go*, because the actual range of angles is restricted by the game's rules. Technically, ATA regulations permit a target to be legally thrown within a maximum arc at the trap of 94 degrees. But while ATA rules allow this wide field for the bird's flight, in practice most traps are stopped so that the total arc of the field is no more than 44 degrees, as the "preferred" limits. The edges of this field are straightaway shots at Stations 1 and 5.

This creates maximum lateral swings of only 22 degrees to either side of the straightaway target from

TRAPFIELD LAYOUT

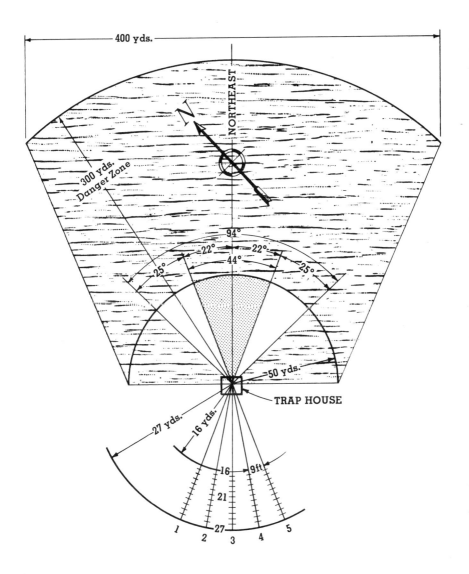

Regulation trapfield layout and angles.

Station 3. A shooter can thus subdivide the entire field of 44 degrees into three basic target flight paths, the two extreme angles with the straightaway between them. The angles or flight paths in between can be considered as variations on the three basic angles. These angles remain constant; only their relationship to the shooter changes as he moves from one station to the next. Thus it is only at Station 3 that the apparent angles and actual angles coincide.

The normal sequence of actions in breaking a target is usually described about like this: The shooter calls for the target; the target becomes visible and its projected path is determined; the shotgun is swung onto it until the barrel has passed ahead of the target; the decision to pull the trigger is made and executed, but the swing continues until the shot hits the target; the target falls away in a burst of pieces; the swing is slowed and halted.

The performance described above sounds simple, and it looks even simpler when skillfully executed. But two of the most crucial ingredients have been omitted, because they must be anticipated and "programmed" even before the shooter calls for the bird. The first is the shooter's position in relation to the traphouse; the second is his gun's starting point of aim. Because the range of possible target angles is different from each of the five stations, the shooter's foot and body positions and his holding points must vary accordingly.

The variations in foot placement and holding point are only slight, from station to station, but they are important. The general rule on foot placement is that the left foot points at about the left back corner of the trap-house on Stations 1 and 2, and towards the right back corner at Stations 4 and 5, with Station 3 in between. This is the general rule, but some shooters modify it slightly in order to adapt it to their own particular style or degree of body flexibility. The basic holding point is a foot above the left corner of the house for Station 1, 18 inches above dead center for Station 3 and a foot above the right corner for Station 5, with Stations 2 and 4 fitting in between. Again, some shooters prefer to hold farther off the house laterally at both Stations 1 and 5, and some like to hold higher. Each shooter must find out what works best for his particular set of muscles and re-flexes, and if holding off the house helps you, it's fine by me.

A word of warning, however: By holding too far off the house you anticipate an angle you may never get, and you run the risk of shortening your swing so much that you impair your follow-through. I personally do best if I hold just barely inside the house at Stations 1 and 5, about halfway to the center of the house at Stations 2 and 4 and dead-center for Station 3, and believe that most shooters are better advised to work on improving their swing than to always be worrying about compensating for a presumed weakness. Now, let's look at the Stations in detail, one by one.

Station 1

From the first peg, the extreme right target is a straightaway, requiring no horizontal lead. The extreme

STATION NO. 1 ANGLES
20 yards = distance average shooter breaks targets

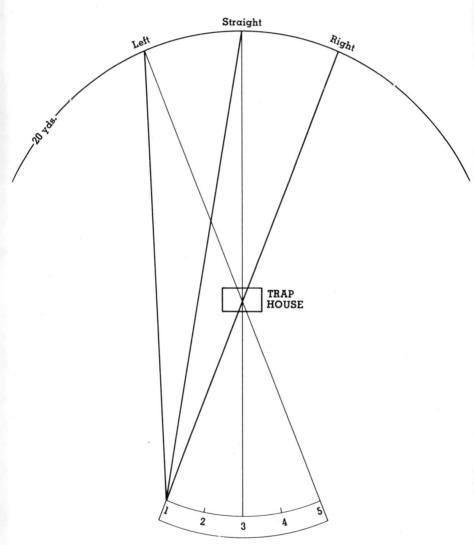

Station 1 angles. The right-hand target is a straightaway,
the left-hand one a hard left-quartering angle.

**The station 1 hold is the left back corner
of the house. I hold about a foot above the house from every peg.**

left bird produces one of the most acute angles in trap-shooting and requires the second longest lead. The computed required lead for an average shooter at this target is approximately three feet, or three gun-barrel widths at the muzzle. For tournament and better-than-average shooters, the lead is usually closer to two feet, because of their quicker reflexes and faster gun swing. The feet are positioned so that the left toe points towards the left back corner of the traphouse.

The actual straightaway shot from the traphouse at this station now becomes a left-quartering shot. If you hold on the left corner of the traphouse, by the time you see the bird and are ready to shoot it, you will have swung the gun up with very little or no lateral swing, depending upon your reaction time. Only a few inches of lead are required.

Station 2

The foot position at this station moves only slightly to the right, if at all, and I like to leave the left toe pointed at the left back corner of the traphouse as it was on Station 1. I do this even though most shooters start favoring the right as soon as they move to the right, reasoning that right-handers swing more naturally to the left, and need help to the right. In practice, however, the most missed bird at Station 2 is the mild left angle which

From Station 2, the hold is inside the left back corner.

resembles the straightaway, and I bet if you'll take my advice and slightly favor the left angle, you'll find it solves this problem.

The extreme right-angle bird from Station 2 is still pretty close to a straightaway, and you can hold slightly to the left of center and raise the gun only a bit to the right to break the right-angle target successfully.

The straightaway from the house is almost the same shot just described, except that the angle is to the left rather than to the right of the traphouse. A lateral lead of less than a foot at the target will usually break the bird.

The hard left-angle shot is a compromise. It isn't as difficult to catch as the same angle from Station 1, but still is not as easy as a straightaway from the house on Station 3. The actual hold on the house from this station is somewhere between the left corner of the house and its center, varying with the personal preference developed by the shooter.

Station 3

At Station 3, because the actual and apparent angles from the traphouse are the same, we have one less variable to contend with. At this station, the three basic target paths are a straightaway, and left and right quartering birds that fly down the extreme sides of the trap's limitations, or what would be straightaways at Stations 1 and 5. The shooter faces the traphouse with his toes so aligned that a line from the tip of the right shoe passing through the tip of the left and extended into the field

STATION NO. 3 ANGLES

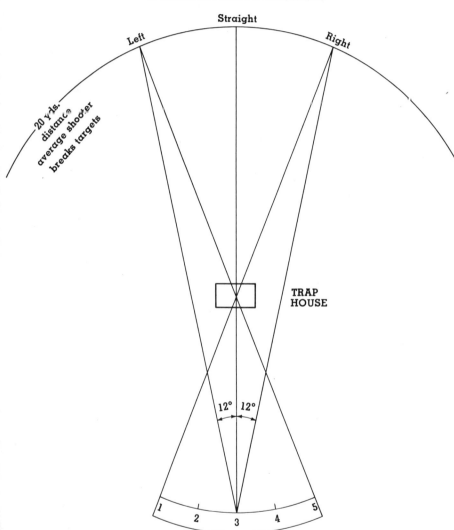

Station 3 angles. The straightaway from this peg looks like "duck soup" to the novice trapshooter, but actually it's the most frequently missed target in the game.

At Station 3 I hold one to two feet above the center of the house.

would parallel the flight of a straightaway bird from Station 5.

At Station 3, most shooters should hold either on the center or just to the right of the center of the house. Those that prefer to hold to the right of the house do so because this hold gives them an earlier peek at the bird if it is a straightaway. Otherwise, the barrel of the shotgun will obscure the target until it rises above the muzzle. The price is a slightly longer swing if the bird is a left-angle target.

The hold above the roof of the house varies from one to two feet for most shooters on Station 3. At Station 1 and all other stations, my hold is about a foot above the house because a higher hold would obscure the target too long. Station 3 is the only peg at which a 2-foot hold is possible, though even a hold directly on the center of the house is allowable. It will take a fraction of a second longer to see the bird with a high hold, but since the gun will move through a shorter rise to meet the target, it tends to reduce the chance of overleading.

The maximum lead for quartering birds is about three feet at Stations 1 and 5. These same angles from Station 3 require only half that, less than two gun barrel widths at most and often no apparent lead. This sense of no apparent lead is what makes these targets a bit deceptive. They are halfway between a straightaway and a quartering shot. If you read them as a straightaway or a slight modification thereof, you might be a bit short on lateral lead. If you are pointing properly, a hint to your poor reading will be a target that jumps to the right when hit. This shows that you are to the left of the bird. The same is true for birds on the left side of center. You tend to shoot at the target instead of where you expect it to be when the shot reaches it. Correct the lead.

Station 4

Station 4 is a compromise between Stations 3 and 5. The hard-right birds aren't as difficult as at 5 since shooters usually don't stop their swing, and thus successfully break the target. The hard-left bird is almost a straightaway with a little drift to the left. Pattern spread usually takes care of any lateral lead required. The actual straightaway out of the house is almost the same target as the hard-left bird out of the house. The difference is

The Station 4 hold: just inside the right back corner.

the direction, a mild right-quartering angle, and the slight hesitancy to swing to the right may make it a notch more difficult than the left bird. Lead on this bird is less than a foot, and sometimes none at all, because the shooter spot-shoots it as far as lateral lead in concerned. The hold on this station is just to the right of the center of the house, or halfway between center and the right corner, and maybe a foot above the roof. What actually happens is that by the time the shooter is ready to fire at the target, it has traveled to the right almost as far as his gun is being held to the right on the house. The lead involved is then only vertical, to get the end of the barrel and target together.

Station 5

Almost everything that occurs at Station 1 holds true, in reverse, at Station 5. However, because a shooter's body coordination tends to favor one side or the other, he cannot swing equally well to either side. Since the majority of shooters are right-handed, they cannot swing quite as well to the right as they can to the left. This makes an extreme right-quartering bird at Station 5 the most difficult target for a majority of shooters. It need not be. The secret is taking a body position that will favor birds traveling to the right on Station 5. This will mean facing off the house for some shooters. However, you should never turn so much to the right that your straight-away shot to the left is fired with the gun across the chest.

Skeet shooters usually have little fear of this station with its extreme angles because they have confidence in their swing. While most trapshooters are aware that this bird requires the maximum of lead, they are so used to shooting the tighter angles that they find it difficult to adjust. Here, again, the problem is often an underlead resulting from stopping the gun when the shooter thinks he is really too far ahead of the bird. Trapshooters can swing as well as skeet shooters—it's just that they don't always believe the leads necessary to break a target and readjust before firing.

The actual straightaway target from the trap-house on Station 5 is a left-quartering bird, similar to the left-quartering bird we met at Station 3. The straightaway is actually a hard-left bird from the house and usually doesn't cause much trouble because it is shot only as a rising bird.

STATION NO. 5 ANGLES

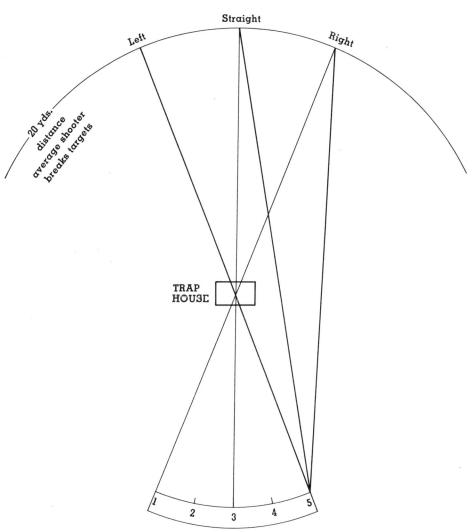

Station 5 angles. Mathematically, the angles here are just like Station 1, and leads would be the same if we could swing as easily to the right as to the left. In practice, however, most right-handers find the right-hand target here a sharper angle than the left-hand bird at Station 1, and use a bit more lead.

Hold on the corner, or slightly outside it, at Station 5.

My normal hold at Station 5 is just above the right corner of the house, but as I've mentioned, some shooters prefer to hold farther to the right than this to favor the hard right-angling target. In general, your hold here will simply be the logical extension of where you've been holding on the other four stations.

Figuring the Wind

Once you've learned the basic positions, leads and timing that work best for you, you wouldn't need anything else—if it weren't for wind. But since wind isn't all that unusual in the United States, and you might have to shoot some day in anything from a gentle breeze to a gale, let's consider what adjustments you might have to make.

There's no denying that the wind can play tricks with the flight of clay targets. It can make them dance, float, appear to hang in mid-air or dart off in directions that make you really swing to catch them. Some shooters convince themselves that they can't shoot in the wind, feel a jinx coming on and go home. The smart thing is to realize that everyone's game will be off a bit, and adjust.

With a little experience, you can learn to read the wind pretty well, and largely compensate for its effect on the flight of targets. A tail wind from straight behind you will keep the birds from climbing as high as they would on a windless day. It flattens the target's path and in a way is a help, actually making the bird easier to shoot. The only warning here is not to overlead the vertical rise, especially on straightaways.

If it's a head wind, one coming straight toward you from the trap, the birds will rise higher than normally. This means that you must increase your normal vertical lead, even to the point of covering up the target with the muzzle. The farther the bird travels, the greater will be the increase in rise. Your best defense here is to get on the birds sooner, before they feel the full effect of the wind, and break them while their trajectory is still more or less uniform.

Quartering winds will give you more trouble than head or tail winds. If the wind is from the right, birds traveling to the right will rise higher and birds to the left side will rise less than normally. Straightaways will also take a slightly different route, with an increasing tendency to drift as they get farther away from the traphouse. Here, again, the best adjustment is to try to get onto the birds faster, and break them before the wind's effect becomes too pronounced.

When the winds are from the left quarter, the conditions become opposite to those described above. Winds from angles in between should be considered accordingly. If the wind is fairly steady, it can be adjusted for well enough for scores to stay close to average. But when the wind is really gusty, changing velocity quickly and shifting—even turning 180 degrees, back and forth —well, go as far as positive thinking can take you, and then try prayer.

7 *Handicap & Doubles Trap*

Shooters who are proficient enough at 16 yards to break a lot of straights sometimes tend to find the challenge fading, yet at the same time they're good enough to discourage less experienced shooters from competing with them on level terms. The handicap system was devised to solve just this problem. It operates by means of distance—in other words, by pushing the better shooter farther and farther back from the traphouse until distance has wiped out his advantage over the less experienced shooter.

Handicap distances start at 18 yards, and run all the way back to 27 yards, the experts' domain known as "shooting from the fence." The classification table below will usually place a shooter of moderate experience behind the 18-yard line, somewhat more skillful shooters at from 19 to 21 yards and the dead-eyes from 22 yards on back.

CLASS	SHOOTER'S AVERAGE AT 16-YARD RISE	HANDICAP YARDAGE
Class AA	96.5 percent and over	24 to 27 yards
Class A	94% and under 96.5%	22 or 23 yards
Class B	91% and under 94%	20 or 21 yards
Class C	88% and under 91%	18 or 19 yards
Class D	Under 88%	16 yards

Yardage handicaps can prove a bit awkward for clubs with a small membership. A man at 18 yards would have a difficult time concentrating with guns going off behind him at 27 yards. Safety considerations, not to mention concentration, have caused several other handicap systems to develop. The most common alternative method involves targets rather than yardage. The shooter is handicapped a given number of birds depending upon his previous average. Based on a hundred targets, a shooter with an average of 96 would be handicapped 12 points; 80 x 100—20 points; 70 x 100—28 points; and 60 x 100—38 points. The poorer the shooter, the smaller his percentage of handicap.

Normal handicap shooting, from 18 yards or more, involves more psychological change than actual physical difference until the shooter moves back behind the 22-yard line. Distances short of this point aren't great enough to require compensation. The only real change is in the shooter's mental approach. He feels that he must shoot differently because he is farther away from the target. Secondly, he tends to try harder, and overdoes it. A new handicap shooter gets the impression that the better shooters, farther back on the line, are watching him critically. Real concentration is necessary, but you must concentrate on shooting just the way you always have. Everyone gets stage fright, and only concentration and experience will help you overcome it.

One thing that shouldn't change as you move back is your timing. There is a tendency of shooters who are first moved back to yardage positions to try to speed up their timing. This shouldn't be necessary. A good shooter at 16 yards will already be taking his birds well before they top their rise, and this habit will pay off at back yardages. Of course, a shooter who consistently takes birds at the top of their rise at 16 yards will have trouble from back yardages. But he shouldn't try simply to shoot faster, and end up pulling the trigger before he's on the bird—the secret is not to shoot faster, but just *swing* faster, move after the bird faster.

Only when you step on the 23-yard line do you begin to require subtle adjustments in gun fit, hold on the house, lead on rising and angling birds and, most of all, in mental attention and concentration.

Once you move to the "back of the fence," three things will immediately become apparent to you. First, you seem to be overextending the range of your shotgun.

Forget it. Your shotgun can do everything called upon it all the way back to 27 yards with no difficulty. Modern shotshells have increased the range of your shotgun. Patterns nowadays are more evenly distributed because of plastic shot collars and special wads. There are fewer holes and less stray shot than ever before.

Your second impression is that the target is smaller and more difficult to pick up quickly than it was from the 16-yard line. It may be a bit smaller, but it is still there and you can see it just as soon if you discipline yourself to make a faster pickup.

Thirdly, your depth perception seems to fall off. In actuality, this is more apparent than real. Stereo vision fades quite quickly, once an object is more than six feet in front of you, and there is relatively little depth discrimination at distances beyond that. So, the change back beyond 16 yards is mostly imaginary. The move appears to sharpen angles more than they actually increase.

Most shooters stick with the same shotgun at handicap yardages that they use at 16 yards. Those who do switch go to a straighter stock, with less drop at comb, because it will provide a higher center of impact. They want a higher comb to adjust for the greater vertical lead. At 16 yards, the computed vertical lead was 7 inches. At 20 yards, it's only two inches more—too little to adjust for. At 27 yards, however, it's half a foot higher than when you were shooting up front. Still, pattern should be sufficient to cover this change in vertical lead even if you don't compensate for it, which makes the use of another gun for this reason alone a little frivolous. I'd stay with your same gun, unless you've been using a less-than-full-choke barrel. In that case, you'd better switch to a tighter choke. Even if you still manage to break targets at the longer distances, you'll slice and chip enough of them to spoil your concentration at a time when you need it most.

The way you address the traphouse from long yardage will be less critical than it was at 16 yards because the amount of swing you need becomes progressively less as you move backwards. Your stance and position are still the same but you'll find your movements smaller, verging on abruptness. (You must be careful here, because abruptness can lead to jerking.)

At longer yardages, however, many top shooters do hold lower on the house. At first, this seems just opposite to what should be done. After all, the angle of rise is greater from back distances because the shooter is moving farther away from the traphouse. If the bird moves higher, then why not hold higher to produce a shorter swing? In reality, your swing is already shortened. From a back distance, a one-inch swing of the barrel covers more distance along the target's flight path than it did at 16 yards. You have in effect, shortened the necessary swing.

The lower hold is recommended because shooters are used to swinging a fixed distance to catch a rising bird. That same swing from back yardages would put them high above the target. The lower hold has the effect of putting the overswing before the bird, rather than after the bird.

Angles also appear sharper, and they are. However, the degree of increase is partly an optical illusion, due to diminishing depth perception. Lead increase should occur, but it should not exceed 18 to 24 inches in front of the target. The maximum 16-yard lead for the average shooter from Station 5 for a hard-right bird is approximately three feet. The one-inch width of your barrel at 16 yards produced a lead at the target of one foot, so you led the bird three barrel-widths. From this same station at 27 yards, the actual lead ahead of the bird should seldom exceed five feet. From 27 yards, the width of the barrel at the target is closer to two feet and the apparent lead is still three barrel-widths.

What it all boils down to, is that if a shooter is shooting properly at 16 yards, you cannot really handicap him by moving him backwards unless he fails to make the proper psychological adjustment. The only real physical difference is that handicap shooting is done at a faster pace than at 16 yards because less swing is required to move the gun on and past the target.

Doubles Trap

Doubles trap is shot from the 16-yard line, usually in strings of 25 or 50 pairs. Instead of one target, two targets are thrown at the same instant. Unlike 16-yards singles, the trap angles are fixed and the two targets travel straightaway courses from Stations 1 and 5, respectively.

Trap doubles always finds fewer shooters participating. This is unfortunate, for while doubles is admittedly more difficult than single trap, it's far more interesting as well as more rewarding. The singles shooter apparently thinks that one target at a time is tough enough to handle, and that two would be too hard. But it isn't. Actually, doubles is more like a combination of singles and handicap trap—the first target is like a singles straightaway, and the second like a handicap shot from 27 yards.

Doubles angles can legally be thrown in an area from 22 to 65 degrees right and left of a straightaway from Station 3. This means a target can legally be in an arc 47 degrees wide. Most traps, however, are set rather close to the 22 degree mark so that one is always a straightaway from Station 1, the other a straightaway from Station 5. Station 3 is the hardest to shoot for most gunners because both birds are angling shots. Stations 2 and 4 are quite similar to 1 and 5 and most shooters treat them that way, taking one bird almost as a straightaway, and the other as an angling shot.

The sixty-four dollar question is which bird to take first. There are two schools of thought on this, and perhaps neither has an overwhelming advantage. The selection usually depends upon which method a shooter uses most naturally and shoots with best. However, I prefer and recommend shooting the straightaway target first and the quartering bird second, from every station.

On Station 1, the right bird is the straightaway and the left bird the quartering target. This sequence stays the same on Stations 2 and 3. At Station 4, the sequence changes, since the bird more closely approaching the straightaway will be the left bird, and it is now taken first. The right bird is quartering and is shot second. On Station 5, the left bird, shot first, is usually a true straightaway while the right bird quarters to the extreme and is taken second.

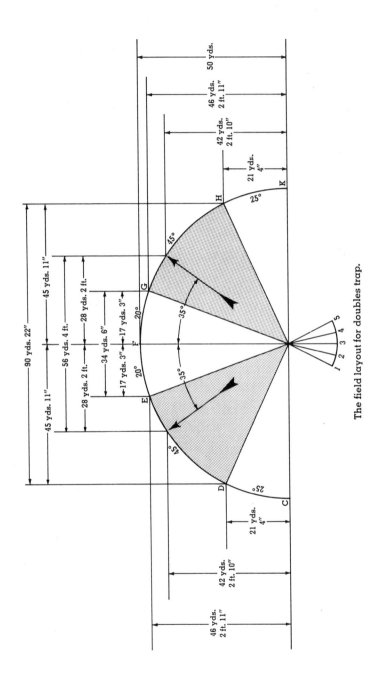

The field layout for doubles trap.

The advantage of this method is that the first bird can be shot very quickly, giving the shooter more time to deal with his second target. On Stations 4 and 5, where he is swinging in his less natural direction, he will find that the extra time more than compensates for the disadvantage of swinging to the right.

The second method takes into account the fact that right-handed shooters swing better to the left than to the right. When using it, the right hand target is shot first from every station so that the more distant bird can be shot with the more comfortable, right-to-left swing. This counteracts the tendency for right-handers to lift their eyes or head in picking up the second target from Stations 4 and 5. However, I'd rather see you work on correcting this tendency instead of trying to avoid it.

Because the flight path of the target in doubles is known, the shooter can ready himself for the first bird of every pair so that little swing will be required. If you stood on Station 3, shooting straightaways, you could point the gun to the area of impact every time and as you became used to it, eventually break the target very close to the house.

This, in effect, is what you must accomplish. The first bird should be taken as quickly as possible, yet not hurried; then concentration can shift to the second bird. The second bird is almost a clear lateral lead. By the time you swing and get onto it, its degree of rising has almost stopped and the pitch of the gun and pattern of the shot will take care of the vertical lead required to break the target. Thus, the key to a good doubles shooting score is the ability to establish a timing that works. There need

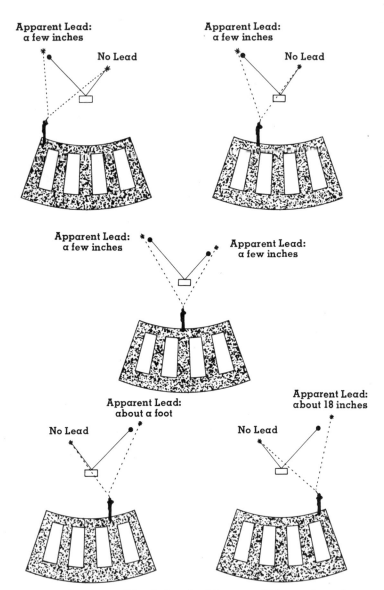

Angles and leads for doubles trap. I like to shoot the straightaway first, which makes you go after the bird that needs swing anyway.

be no loss of time incurred by an unknown target-path, and this makes up for the swing-time needed on the second bird. The birds should still both be taken on the rise. Since your first shot in doubles should always be the target most nearly approaching the straightaway, your holding point on the house should favor this target. Exactly where this will be depends on the particular kind of targets the trap is throwing. However, unless you're shooting first in the squad, you can "go to school" on the shooter ahead of you and know pretty accurately where yours will appear.

Slightly different body coordination and positioning is demanded in doubles. The swing after the second bird is greater than even the most extreme angles at singles. In singles, your position splits the swing-area in half. But in doubles, you know the birds will always be at the extremes. Position becomes doubly important. The rule is usually to take a position that is most favorable to breaking the second bird, a position slightly to the right of what would would be a fair compromise for breaking both birds, acknowledging that the swing to the left is easier.

Stance, too, must be modified slightly for doubles because of the recoil factor. The shooter must place his weight just a bit more forward than when shooting singles. This helps to compensate for the recoil of the first shot and speeds the shooter's recovery for the second shot. After recoil, he pushes forward again, though not quite as much as the first time. As he does so, he unwinds his body from the waist to swing after the second bird. The greater movement from the waist is needed because the arc the gun must move through is too great to be accomplished smoothly by moving the arms and shoulders alone.

To shoot doubles, you obviously need a shotgun that can dependably fire two shots. Most serious doubles shooters use an over-and-under because of its single sighting plane and positive functioning, but you'll also see many autoloaders. The side-by-side double makes it easier to lose a target by covering up the bird with its width, but the Winchester 21 is still my personal preference. Admittedly it's a minority choice.

While most shooters prefer their guns choked Full-and-Full, and this is what I do, others like to have the first barrel they shoot at a straightaway slightly more open. They feel they can almost "point-shoot" the first target and get onto the second before it travels too far. The second barrel, in any case, is always full-choked.

Some shooters shoot the same load in both barrels. However, I like to mix them, using the light $2\frac{3}{4}$-dram load in the first barrel (normally with No. 8 shot) and a 3-dram load in the second barrel. I like the light load in the first barrel so that recoil won't throw off the second shot. It just means keeping your shells in different pockets, which is a simple thing to become accustomed to.

8 *Improving Your Shooting*

Improvement in trapshooting depends on practice and an intelligent analysis of your errors. Without the latter the former is almost useless—you only perfect the fault, making it that much harder to correct later on. Oh, I realize that some shooters develop means of compensating for faults that enable them to shoot high scores even though the fault remains, but it's the long way around—it takes longer, requires much more natural talent and never really produces as good a result in the end.

Since I've spent the best part of my life teaching

If you hit a bad slump, don't be too proud
to get help, instead of trying to fight your
way out all by yourself. But be choosy
about the kind of help you look for!
Spotting flaws and knowing how to correct
them are two different things, and lots of
good shooters can't do either.

shotgunners, it shouldn't surprise you to find that I think
the best way to learn and improve is to get your basic
foundation from a first-class professional coach, and then
have periodic checkups to keep your practice on the right
track. I've seen too many mediocre shots who've taught
themselves or have been "helped" by friends to have much
confidence in these approaches, and I really believe that
lessons from an expert are the best, fastest and cheapest
way to improve your shotgunning. Of course, this alter-

native just isn't practical for a lot of shooters, and they have no choice but to ask fellow shooters for advice, or try to help themselves.

Unless you're really lucky, it's usually easier to get another shooter to teach you his faults than it is to get him to correct yours. Teaching is a special talent, and even if a man has a gift for it, he doesn't learn how to teach overnight. Too many shooters end up with a whole collection of quirks and gimmicks they've picked up from other shooters, but no real foundation. On balance, you're probably better off taking a book like this one and trying to work it out yourself.

It's especially important, if your improvement is going to depend entirely on your own efforts, to take the time to set up a specific program for yourself—if not on paper, then at least in your mind. This is a serious step in the scheme of improving. Next, find a club or range where you can shoot consistently. If you are only going to shoot a half-dozen times a year, you can't ever really hope to progress very far. Even if you've decided that you'll shoot every weekend, join a club with a league that will further motivate you to shoot more regularly. Regular, consistent shooting is the first essential for improving your score.

How much should you shoot? Every chance you get, and as much as you can afford. In fact, in the beginning I'd almost advise you to shoot more than you could afford as a steady diet. Give up some other pleasure temporarily so that you can shoot often enough to remember what you learn. *You learn by repetition.* Shoot often enough to be able to remember what you learn, and start breaking enough targets to develop some confidence in your own ability. Once you have learned that you can break a good score, you need shoot only often enough to keep in practice, and this, of course, varies with the individual.

Shooting one or two days a week may be all the time you can devote, and this is certainly better than nothing. However, the best approach to improving your shooting is to try to shoot every other day, perhaps in the evening, for a week, ten days or two weeks. Fairly intensive shooting, closely spaced, is often more beneficial than the same amount more widely spaced. With weekend shooting, it often takes a couple of rounds for a shooter to get in the groove, and by then it's already time to quit. When shooting every other day, you can pick up the groove much more quickly, and start shooting your best sooner. The ideal way is to shoot every day for a week, and then take a week off. Seven days of shooting in a row will do far more than seven weekends of one-day shooting. You'll mark your progress almost from day to day.

In fact, you should keep a written record of your self-improvement program so that you can follow the progress of your scores and average, and see how well you're really doing. When weather conditions adversely affect your scores, make a notation in your trap log so that you can take that into consideration. It's also helpful to keep track of the birds you drop, and the particular points you were concentrating on when you shot the round. By the end of any given period you can then recapitulate, and quite possibly detect the pattern your future practice emphasis ought to take.

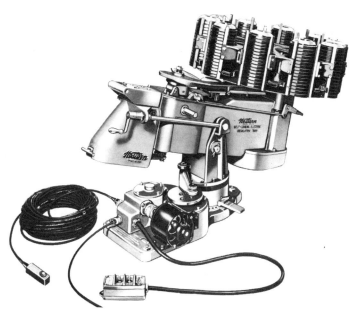

This is what a modern trap looks like. If
you're lucky, it's the kind you have to
practice over—it's the only one made that
can be locked in any position, a great
advantage in working out problem angles.

Most practice, of course, involves developing and
maintaining a good "groove" of habitual form and timing, and gives the shooter a chance to experiment a bit
and find out just what personal adjustments and variations work best for him. For it goes without saying that no
two shooters are *exactly* alike. We can generalize about
average shooters, or normal ones or median ones statisti-
cally, but that's all they are—statistics. You're a particu-

lar individual, with your own dimensions and reflexes and timing, and you have to learn how to adjust the generalizations that work for this "average" shooter until they work for you, too. Perhaps you swing fast enough, naturally, to break most birds with less apparent lead than most shooters require. Fine. Or you may need more apparent lead—it's just as easy to compensate, as long as you recognize which way to go for you.

Normally, a right-handed shooter can swing best to the left. But maybe you shouldn't hold as far to the right on Station 5 as is often recommended. Perhaps you can hold a little more to the left and still handle the right-angling birds just as well. Test it methodically. If you find that you must hold a little more to the left on one station, you may want to adjust all your holds on all your stations a bit more to the left.

So go ahead and experiment—with timing, with leads, with where you hold on the house, with foot position, with gun fit—but do it methodically, and only change one variable at a time, so that you can keep track of what you're finding out.

If you have been missing a bird from one particular station and angle, duplicate it in practice, and fix the trap at that angle. Keep shooting until you consistently break it well. While only Winchester makes an automatic trap that can be locked in any position, almost all traps can be locked in at least two or three positions. Even this can be helpful if you want to determine your leads.

As an example, straightaways at Station 3 are missed by more shooters than any other targets. If you want to work on it, lock the trap in that position and shoot an entire box of shells from there. Similarly, if you're having troubles with the hard-left-angle bird from Station 1 or the hard-right-angle bird from Station 5, lock the trap in those positions and start shooting. Your problem is probably one of incorrect lead. By steadily increasing it you can get the sight-picture of the correct lead imprinted in your mind. You can even try leading farther and farther until you miss by overleading. (You'll be amazed at the amount of swing necessary to accomplish this.)

Another good exercise is to start at Station 3, call for a few straightaway birds and then slowly change the angle of the trap to the left, so that you can observe exactly how much the lead must be increased as the angle grows. Then move over to the right and watch the lead slowly grow ahead of the birds angling off to that side. The problem with angling targets is that your sub-conscious mind keeps telling you to shoot *at* the target, and it takes conscious effort to learn to shoot *ahead* of it. When you have learned the correct sight picture in this manner, however, you seldom forget it.

Always notice how you're breaking your birds. Good breaks are "puffed," "powdered" or otherwise smashed into a lot of small pieces. If you are slicing birds, then a little analysis can help you. Many shooters, even those who shoot a lot and shoot well, are not aware that you can analyze where you are pointing, where the point of impact occurs, just from the kind and number of pieces into which the targets are broken. A good point produces a powdered bird. But if you break only one or two pieces from a bird, either you are not centering your pattern properly or your timing is off. In almost every sliced bird, the fragments of target will fly away from the point of impact. If a small piece of clay flies upward and the big chunk is sent low, you have topped the bird, or shot above it. If the big piece jumps upward on the break, then you were under the bird. If the main fragments snap off and travel to the left, you were to the right of the bird, and only the left part of your pattern was on the target. The opposite is true on the other side.

The shooter has never lived who *always* shoots the same. Fatigue, both physical and mental, takes its toll, and you don't always get up on the same side of the bed. But a good shooter will be able to analyze where he is shooting. As this changes slightly, from day to day or even hour to hour, he'll make adjustments, taking his clue from the way he's breaking his targets. After the first five or ten birds, every shooter should determine if his pointing is slightly off-center or if his timing is off and compensate for the error.

But while you should adjust, promptly and accurately, you should never change your basic style of shooting without a reason. You should change only if you are doing something wrong and want to improve it, or if you are experimenting with a variation of stance, hold or pointing. Generally, you should never shoot one way for practice and fun and then try to shoot another way for competition. Always shoot with a purpose, and do the best within your capabilities. Goofing off or sloppy shooting can result in bad habits as well as poor scores.

Practice sessions are the logical place to try out different guns, if you have serious doubts about your own, and within limits, you can also try different stock dimensions by adding tape to the comb, switching recoil pads and so on. Trapshooting is so full of variables as it is, however, that you're usually wiser to eliminate as many as you can; try to settle on a gun so that your main emphasis can be on improving your skills and performance instead of your equipment. Especially avoid trying strange guns and making compensations for them. Very often the compensation will rub off onto your style even after you've switched back to your regular gun.

If you're a good shoooter, don't be too quick to take a new gun as a permanent partner on the basis of a good practice score or two. Remember, shooters often concentrate harder with a strange gun, and it takes quite a few shots before you start to become thoroughly accustomed. In the meantime, if your scores are a bit higher, you'll be tempted to credit the new gun instead of your own greater concentration, only to find in time that you're still the same shooter, and that your "ol' faithful" wasn't so bad after all. Remember, guns don't go sour, shooters do; don't blame the gun for the bad habits you pick up!

9 *Trapshooting Psychology*

In any competitive activity—football, track, golf or even business—the key to success lies in eliminating, as nearly as possible, those physical factors that could cause you to fail. Physical factors make up 90 percent of a winning effort. The remaining 10 percent depends on psychological factors, mostly on concentration. Thus if you can gain control of the physical factors, you can put all of your effort into concentrating.

In football, for example, the player gets into top condition, gets the right shoes, pads and uniform, applies black under his eyes to prevent glare, studies and practices his plays until he knows them as well as he knows his own name. This leaves him free, once the game has started, to concentrate all of his energies on what his opponent is doing.

Business deals, even the biggest ones, are much the same. If you have complete command of all of your own facts and figures and have eliminated as far as possible any chance of a physical mistake, you can concentrate on what your opponent is doing and perfectly meet his every move. In other words, winning is generally simply a case of striving for perfection yourself, and letting your opponent make the mistakes.

The first eight chapters of this book have been concerned with helping you to control the physical factors involved in trapshooting so that you can eliminate the mistakes that can keep you from winning. Such things as position, stance, gun fit, equipment and basic style are, after all, physical things that can be easily checked and changed. Winning, however, is an individual psychological thing. Anyone and anything can *help* you win, but nobody can do it for you—you're the only one who can do the actual winning!

Trapshooting is a special kind of competition because it involves not only you against the other shooters, but also you against the target, and success in the second match-up is the key to success in the first. Never forget this, for it must be a primary factor in your thinking. For example, you should never go to a shoot thinking that you'll be the only AA shooter there, and thus ought to win. Until the day that you convince yourself that you can break 100 targets, and that the other shooters, no matter who they are, can do no more, you'll never be a champion.

This is easier said than done. Just let an Arnold Riegger or a Dan Orlich walk on the grounds, and two thirds of the shooters are ready to give up. This is a natural reaction, and it's tough to control—but control it you must, if you expect to win.

You can teach a shooter everything except the will to win. This he must have himself. It may be only a spark that someone else must help to fan into a flame, as I have done many times with my pupils, but the spark must be there. If you do not have this feeling about competition, then forget about competitive shooting. This will to win is intimately related to your belief in yourself, in your *confidence* that you can break every target. You must be able to convince yourself that the 400th and 500th targets are no different from the first, and be able to stay relaxed enough to break them. This is the only way to control pressure. It works like this: The more confidence you have, the more targets you break, and the more targets you break, the easier it becomes. The easier it becomes, the more confidence you have. Now let's consider some special problems and ways of overcoming them.

Slumps

As long as your misses are pretty well distributed, in terms of the station and type of shot, improving your overall concentration is the best way to improve your score. But most of the better shooters find that their dropped birds tend to come from a certain "difficult" angle, or even a difficult station. Well, let me tell you something. There's no such thing as a difficult *target*—it's the shooter who has the difficulty. Usually your difficult target is simply a station at which your technique is shaky, because you can't remember (or perhaps never knew) the best way to deal with it. Technical insecurity is quickly reflected in loss of confidence, and wherever you lack confidence on the field, that's where your difficult target will be.

The real trouble is that concern about a difficult target rarely stops there. Worrying about it makes you miss some other target you *know* how to hit, and thinking about that miss makes you drop yet another bird. You start to wonder if something much more basic isn't wrong, and you hesitate, or change your timing. You become so anxious to see whether or not you've broken the target that you start to lift your eyes, and then your head. Before you know it, you're not only having trouble with a difficult bird—you're getting where you can't be sure of breaking anything from that station, or from any other.

And that's not the worst phase, either. Confidence and poise can be so completely destroyed that I've seen shooters snap-shoot at the air, before the bird was visible, and I've also seen them when they couldn't pull the trigger at all. I've seen "old smoothies" turn into apparent spastics. Few shooters are capable of bailing themselves out by analyzing their own problems at this stage. They're too close to the problem to see it, and they're better off hollering for help—not just to anybody, but to a pro. An experienced coach can save you a lot of time and anguish, in most cases, because he can identify the problem so much more quickly than the average skilled shooter.

But even when you know exactly what you're doing wrong, as a result of either self-analysis or outside help, it can still be a problem to correct it. Let me tell you a secret: Very often the answer lies in redirecting your attention *away* from *hitting* the target, and focusing it instead on what *you are doing* to hit the target, i.e., onto the movements that lead to the breaking of the bird.

In other words, go back to the fundamentals and concentrate on them, especially on the positive act that corrects the flaw that has worked its way into your form. Take the time to run down the whole list of basics— stance, position, gun-mounting, aiming points—and make certain that none of the basics has gone awry. Nine times out of ten one of them has, and nine times out of ten that's what you eventually pay the coach for hammering back into your skull.

The worst thing you can do with a bad slump is to try to "shoot your way out" by blindly continuing and simply hoping that something will change. This is the first thing the novice shooter tries, and it's about the last thing that ever works. The next thing he usually tries is some gimmick, some unorthodox wrinkle. This is going in exactly the wrong direction. When you're having trouble, concentrate on fundamentals and try to come back to a style that's *more* orthodox, not less. Any coach will tell you that's the best way to put the odds back in your favor.

Release triggers

While we're on the subject of slumps, confidence and fundamentals, we might as well discuss release triggers—the special trap triggers that do not fire when pulled, but only when released. To me, they belong here and not in the chapter on hardware, for I believe that they have more to do with the shooter's psychology than they do with mechanics. Sure, some shooters claim they prefer the release trigger not because they've got a problem, but because it enables them to shoot faster, takes less energy or gives them a better chance to correct if they come up to a target wrong. The alleged faster lock time is supposed to give you a second chance.

Other shooters adopt release triggers quite frankly as a crutch, as a means of compensating for flinching, snap-shooting or being unable to pull the trigger at all. No doubt sometimes the release trigger helps these things for some shooters. Some fine scores are shot with release triggers, just the way some fine shooters use funny stances, and I'd certainly never disparage the mechanical ingenuity and craftsmanship of the gunsmiths who install them. Nonetheless, my experience has taught me that the release trigger is just another place to go, in attempting to solve a problem, instead of the right place. In my view, if your problem is flinching, go to lighter loads, or correct your gun fit or try an autoloader—do whatever is necessary to correct the *actual* cause, if it's in any way physical.

What if it's psychological or emotional? I'd still rather try to find out why, and tackle it head-on, than to look for an answer elsewhere. If your timing gets too jumpy, try to learn to pace yourself and slow it down. If you get the "yips" because you're not psychologically ready to shoot the target, the release trigger can't make up your mind for you—the thing to change is you, not your trigger mechanism.

Timing and Tension

Good timing depends on knowing what you're doing and having confidence in your own ability. There's no way to "make sure" that you're going to break the target. Quite the contrary—the longer you hesitate, trying to make sure of the target, the bigger risk you run of losing it. There's only one right time to pull the trigger: the very first instant that the muzzle and the bird are in the right relationship. As soon as you are "on" the target, *shoot!* Why wait? This failure to shoot until it's actually too late is a common fault, even among fairly good shooters. They aren't alert enough to realize that they are on top of the target as quickly as they actually are. Or they let tension paralyze them.

Tension is undeniably a big factor in trapshooting. When you're going for your first "straight" or your first 50 or 100 straight, or your first handicap straight, right on up to the shoot-off for the Grand American, tension is going to be there, and it's going to be building as the race progresses. It's a factor, yes, but it shouldn't be a problem. For tension is a wonderful thing, if you can learn to put it to work for you. Tension can keep you alert during a long shoot-off, sharpen your powers of observation, keep your reflexes razor sharp—nothing, in fact, can help your concentration more than tension. The secret is learning how to stay loose physically at the same time. If there's one attribute top-notch competitors in all sports have in common, it's that—the ability to get keyed up mentally while staying relaxed physically. Perhaps that's all that concentration really is: getting keyed up while staying relaxed.

Squadding

One of the most immediate influences on the shooter's state of mind and his timing is the other shooters on his squad, and serious shooters try to pick their squad partners carefully. Good shooting is contagious, and the safest rule to go by, when squadding-up, is to seek shooters with better ability than your own. The temptation is often the opposite. Nobody likes to be embarrassed by showing up as the low man in a squad, and sometimes it seems safer to pick a squad in which you can shine. But when you shoot with better shooters, you'll tend to pick up their timing, and even though it may seem too fast to you, often when the scores are tallied you'll find you've been shooting over your head. Conversely, novice and low-average shooters are usually characterized by poor timing and non-rhythmic shooting, and when this is the dominant pattern, it can be catching, too. Thus poorer shooters usually benefit from shooting with a better squad, while the isolated good shooter will suffer (though to a lesser degree) from shooting with novices.

"Jinxes"

The shooter who has learned to discipline his concentration should be able to shoot well under all conditions. However, this doesn't mean that he shouldn't eliminate variables when possible, if it makes his shooting easier. For example, some shooters have found that they shoot better at one time of day rather than another. The early birds feel they can do their very best as close to the crack of dawn as they can get, while others prefer to be up and around for a while, and to see how the other scores are going, before they step to the line.

If you've got no particular preference, it's not a bad idea to base your selection on the characteristic local weather pattern. In some parts of the country, especially the coastal areas, there are often morning winds which fade in the afternoon and pick up again toward dusk. Elsewhere the tendency may be for little wind early in the day, and an increasing wind as the morning progresses. But don't make too much of a thing about trying to outguess the weather—the best you can do, most of the time, is to learn how to handle the wind and hope it proves pretty much the same for everybody.

Just as the time of day affects confidence for some shooters, so does the starting position in the squad for others. Of course, you should be able to shoot equally well from any position, but you might just feel a bit more comfortable starting at one station instead of another. If that sets you at ease and puts you in a better frame of mind, fine. However, never let it get out of hand. Never let it reach the point where you think it's a jinx to start shooting from another station or at another time of day. Don't use it as a crutch. If you do, you're doing something wrong. If you think this is happening to you, start switching before the habit becomes too deeply instilled.

Another jinx is the "long run" bug. A shooter is going great, with a long run of no misses, until because of some minor distraction he loses his concentration and drops a bird. Then he really blows it. He drops the next, and the next and sometimes more. It may take several birds before he reestablishes his concentration. How can he avoid this? Some shooters stop, take a deep breath, relax for a moment, take a step backward and then re-address the traphouse. But whatever you do, don't overdo it. Too much worry or fidgeting can extend the lost-bird run. Reset your feet, bring the gun up smartly and make sure it is fitted into the shoulder pocket. Don't take too long to call for the bird, but don't call for it until you are sure. Then let your habitual shooting pattern take over. Rely on your reflexes, for if you have learned, properly, you'll probably see the bird powder.

"Pull"

How you call for the target is just a detail, but it's still an important one, for the way you call "pull" influences how well the pull will be accomplished. A weak call makes the shooter sound scared (even to himself, per-haps) and is hard for the trap boy to hear. Not quite certain, he will often give a slow pull that can disrupt the shooter's timing. A reasonably sharp, strong "pull" is more than just whistling in the dark, for it not only sounds confident, it assures a good, fast pull by the trap boy. Too loud a call, however, simply wastes energy and tends to annoy the rest of the squad. Some shooters tend to rise in volume, unconsciously, as the tension builds; others do it intentionally, believing that they keep themselves sharp that way. Probably a better way is to treat the call a bit like a rifle shot: when you're ready, inhale, release part of the air and call for the bird. It'll keep your tension under control, and your scores, too.

Practice Rounds

Practice rounds can build you up psychologically for the shoots for record, as long as you treat them like practice rounds. You should always shoot to break targets, and thus shoot seriously. But if you miss during a practice round, realize that you weren't mentally primed to break them all—you were simply loosening your muscles, getting ready for the record shoot. Don't let your practice round score affect the way you will shoot in competition.

Personally, I don't like to shoot an entire practice round before I shoot for record. I do like to take a half-dozen shots or so, just to get the feel of the trigger and the gun so that they won't seem strange when I start shooting. I don't like to shoot a full round as practice, however, because I want to conserve my powers of concentration, and hate to waste a round of 25. There are just so many straights, or 25s, in a man, and I don't like to use them up in practice. Also, if you do go straight you are building up pressure unnecessarily because the 25 you have just shot doesn't count toward your hundred. It means you will actually have to shoot 125 straight to get 100 straight on record.

Whatever you prefer in practice rounds, I'd suggest that you go to the trap where you're going to shoot at least one round before your squad is up. Watch the targets, see what they're doing. How high are they flying, and how does the puller operate? Don't just walk up blind, and step out on the field without knowing what's going on. The shooters who win the silverware take every advantage they can find, even the baby ones.

Shoot-offs

Let's say that one day you do everything right that we've been talking about, and post four 25s on the tournament scoreboard. That's all 100 straight is—four 25s. Not too long ago if you broke them all you could pick up the trophy and go home. But today, we've got more good shooters than ever, and you may very well break 100 only to find yourself tied with a bunch of other hotshots. A tie means just one thing: shoot-off.

So what? If you've got the right psychological approach, shoot-offs are no more difficult than the main event. In fact, I've always told myself that they were actually easier, for the simple reason that once you've made the shoot-off, you no longer have to outshoot several hundred shooters, only the three our four who've also made the shoot-off. You wouldn't be tied with them if you weren't just as good as they are, and you're all going to shoot on the same trap and at the same targets. So all you've got to do is keep doing the right things until the others make a mistake, and be ready to accept their congratulations.

Being ready to do your best in the shoot-off isn't much different from being ready for any other round. Be sure your equipment is ready well in advance, and remember to include your clear glasses—shoot-offs start late and end later. If you shot in an early squad, break a few practice targets half an hour or so before the last squad finishes, just to get the feel of things again. Remember, wind and light conditions may have changed since you broke your 100.

One last bit of advice: get some experience shooting under lights *before* you need to do it for record. Today, many of the big shoots are so well attended that the shoot-offs must be held under the lights, and a shoot-off is not the time to start learning how the lights affect you. Shooting under lights doesn't normally require any great change in your shooting pattern, though when lighting is poor, it sometimes helps to put a little white chalk or a "muzzle bandage" on the end of your barrel. The main thing is to get enough practice under lights in advance for you to have confidence in your ability to break targets under these conditions when you need it. For once you've worked out your basic mechanics and learned how to concentrate, confidence is the real key to winning, with perhaps a little luck thrown in for seasoning. Do everything you can to develop confidence; it may prove all the seasoning you need!

10 *Tournament Shooting*

Trapshooting has its own intrinsic rewards, and shooting just for amusement is all the motivation some trapshooters need to keep them coming back time after time. There's no denying, though, that trapshooting—more than skeet or any other shotgun game—tends to produce a lively spirit of competition in most individuals. And most shooters find, as soon as they're breaking targets with a fair degree of consistency, that the competitive bug has had a chew at them, and that they'd like to measure themselves against some other shooters and per-

Trapshooting is a game everyone can play, as this squad at the 1969 Grand American attests. Furthermore, you can play it for most of your life, and there's no reason to assume that the youngster on Station 2 won't be still breaking targets at Vandalia fifty years from now.

haps even invest a little money on the outcome. Just knowing you can break targets gets to be no longer good enough. You want everyone to know it, and the way to do this is to win tournaments.

The best way to win tournaments is to shoot in tournaments. For heaven's sake, don't pick a state or regional tournament for your debut—begin your competitive shooting at your home club or the nearest club that holds registered shoots. I say "registered" because there is a great psychological difference in knowing whether or not the score you're shooting is "for keeps" or just a casual exercise.

Registered Tournaments

All registered competitions are conducted according to rules laid down by the Amateur Trapshooting Association (ATA), the official governing body for trapshooting in both the United States and Canada. Over the years, the ATA has developed a body of rules and regulations so that trapshoots can be conducted equitably and with organization anywhere in North America. Almost every gun club that intends to hold interclub competitive shoots joins ATA and agrees to abide by its rules. Gun clubs hold shoots in accordance with ATA rules after applying for registration of a specific shoot. The shoot is then listed on a calendar or directory printed in *Trap & Field,* the official publication of ATA. All shooters in the registered event must be individual members of the ATA. The shooter's scores are recorded in the national office, where all records are kept and yearly averages computed.

The records are then used in handicapping and classifying shooters.

Starting out by shooting at your local club will insure that you are shooting among friends, and help build confidence and overcome self-consciousness. After all, "Old Joe" knew you when you couldn't break 15, and he'll be the first to congratulate you when you break 100. But as soon as you're busting them pretty well at your local club, you ought to start branching out at some out-of-town shoots. Shooting away from home creates pressures you won't find on your own field. Breaking 100 straight in your own back yard is one thing, but doing it in someone else's back yard is another proposition.

When you first shoot away from home, take a friend (a shooter, not a lady) with you. "Misery loves company," and your first shoot away from home will probably be rough. A friend will help you laugh it off on the way home. A good way of introducing yourself to the problems of shooting away from home is to join a league that shoots "home and home" meets.

League Shoots

League shooting is something that every shooter who is serious about improving his score should consider. The competitive urge contributes even further to the shooter's desire and motivation to improve his game. Trap leagues operate in much the same manner as other recreational leagues. They can be sponsored by industrial firms, service clubs, unions or various social and fraternal organizations. Other trap leagues are established

The best place to start your competitive
shooting is in interclub or league tournaments. Many local clubs provide facilities
for skeet as well as trap, as does the
Winchester franchised layout at Bethany,
Conn., shown above.

145 Tournament Shooting

between trap clubs with no outside sponsorship and function just as well, if not better. They operate much like golf teams and attain a high standard of serious competition.

For interclub shoots, many organizations make it a practice to designate their five best shooters to the team representing the club, with several as alternate shooters. These shooters have the added advantage of shooting together regularly and developing their team style and timing to a fine edge. Other clubs assign the entire club to a five-man team and all members in rotation are called upon at one time or another to represent their club on a squad. Another variation is for a club to form several squads, one with the old high school varsity designation and a second line of shooters as the junior varsity. Or just several squads with no ability designation compete against an equal number of squads from another club. This type of competition is usually non-league, but matched club shooting.

State Shoots

From league and club contests, a competitor can graduate to state shoots. Each state, district, territory and province has a trapshooting organization that operates in cooperation with ATA. Each area holds an annual shoot to determine champions and awards ATA trophies and state class awards. Class trophies are purchased by the states but can bear ATA emblems. Varying according to the number of events, state shoots last from three to five days and are patterned closely after zone shoots.

Zone Shoots

There are five zones in the United States and Canada for purposes of trapshooting competition and political organization, according to ATA. The Central Zone encompasses those states south and west of the Great Lakes and Manitoba and Saskatchewan. The Eastern Zone includes the District of Columbia and all the states directly north of it, including West Virginia and Maryland as well as Ontario, Quebec and the Maritime Provinces. The Southern Zone includes Alabama, the Bahamas, Florida, Georgia, Kentucky, Mississippi, North Carolina, South Carolina, Tennessee, Virginia and the Canal Zone. The Southwestern Zone is made up of Arkansas, Kansas, Louisiana, Missouri, New Mexico, Oklahoma and Texas. The Western Zone is widest in its scope, and includes Alaska, Arizona, California, Colorado, Hawaii, Idaho, Montana, Nevada, Oregon, Utah, Washington, Wyoming, Alberta and British Columbia.

Each zone annually holds one shoot, usually at a different location each time. Zone champions in shot singles, handicap, doubles and all-around competition are awarded ATA trophies. Trophies are also given for women and juniors and for class champions.

Regulations from the national organization require that singles championships be determined on 200 targets, the handicap on 100 targets and the doubles on championship 100 (50 pairs). The all-around trophy goes to the shooter scoring the highest total on these 400 championship targets. All trophies are open only to residents of that zone.

The Grand American Tournament

The highest rung of the competitive ladder you started climbing at your local club is situated about 10 miles from Dayton, Ohio, and every year towards the end of August, dedicated trapshooters from all over the world come to have a go at scaling it. The Grand American Tournament, our North American and national championship event, takes place at the Vandalia headquarters of ATA over a nine-day period (three days of preliminaries and six days of championship competition) and some three thousand-odd shooters participate, making this the largest such gathering anywhere in the world.

The published program is a fairly complicated one, running to some 32 pages including the roster of past winners at the Grand. Preliminary events last year consisted of three 100-target singles events, three 100-target handicap events, 50 pair of doubles and two 100-target ATA Modified International Clay Pigeon competitions (note the further discussion of this event below). Grand American Week proper begins with Class Championship Day and the Champion of Champions events which are restricted to the first three guns at ATA-registered state or provincial tournaments. The second day is given over to the Double Class Championship and the Ohio Handicap, and the third to the ATA Clay Target Singles Championship of 200 16-yard targets. The prestige of this event is second only to the Grand itself.

The fourth day of Grand American week witnesses the 100-target Preliminary Handicap, and the fifth day the Grand American Handicap of 100 targets itself.

Closing day is devoted to the 100-target Doubles Championship, the 100-target Vandalia Handicap and the big aggregate-score awards, the High Over-All Championship and the All-Around Championship. The first of these is based on the 1,000 program targets shot the whole Grand American week, and the second, on the 400 targets of the Clay Target Championship, the Grand American Handicap and the Doubles Championship.

Of course, quite a few more titles are bestowed during the Grand than the particular championships mentioned above, for in most events there are also Lady, Junior, Sub-Junior, Veteran and Industry titles and trophies and cash awards as well. In fact, quite a little piece of change is collected and distributed at the Grand every year—entrance fees and shells (which must be purchased at the grounds for each event) run from a low of $20 in the preliminaries to a high of $53 in the Grand, including the optional purses. All the entries make a considerable dent in the bank account of a shooter who's below part that week, but my what those purses can do for the man who gets hot at the right time!

Considering how much is at stake, it's surprising how casual many shooters are when they first come to

Overleaf:
Modern trapshooting at its acme: the ATA
grounds at Vandalia as they appear
today. It's a far cry from the scene pictured
on pages 32 & 33.

Vandalia, or perhaps "how naive" is a better way to put it. More than one competitor has tried to spruce up for the big week with a new jacket, a new gun or even new shoes, only to find that he couldn't produce "that old feeling"—or his accustomed scores—while using them. Generally speaking, the Grand American isn't the place to break in a new anything, even though Charles Harvey, who won the Grand in 1970, picked up a new gun on the Wednesday before the event and shot only the 100 Preliminary Handicap targets with it before he won the title. He was pressing his luck, and then some, even with a custom-fitted gun.

The first time I shot at Vandalia I had all my equipment as right as I could get it, but I made another mistake: I forgot just how big that 97-acre layout it, and ended up half sprinting down the line to join my squad on time, shedding most of my self-possession en route. The score I shot thereafter was not one of the ones I enjoy remembering, but I never failed to give myself time for a leisurely stroll thereafter, and the education was worth it. Yes, no matter where you finish, the Grand American is always educational, and if you like to shoot, you really shouldn't figure on being anywhere else in late August.

International Trap (Olympic Trench)

The kind of trapshooting that's competed in internationally and at the Olympic Games is a different form of the game we've been talking about, and in my estimation, the greatest challenge of all. In Olympic-style trapshooting, a 15-trap, ground-level installation is used, the traps being placed in a straight line and divided into five groups of three traps each. The shooting stations are 15 meters directly behind the center trap in each group, and the squad consists of six shooters, five of whom are in firing position at one time. Angles and heights of targets are much greater than the ATA standard, and the bird is a faster bird, since it must fly a minimum of 70 meters.

To permit shooters to cope with these greater difficulties, two shots are permitted at each target, and it makes no difference in scoring if the bird is hit with the first or second shot. Shooters use a bit more shell, with $1\frac{1}{4}$ ounces of shot permitted and no restriction on the powder charge, and the bird is called for with the gun already mounted, like U.S. trap but unlike International Skeet.

Olympic trap is a darned tough game, but a great one. Unfortunately, the investment in traps an international layout requires seems to doom any sizeable or rapid growth of this form of the sport. The first two official 15-trap fields in the United States were at military installations (Fort Benning, Georgia, and San Antonio, Texas), which is not surprising; today there are still fewer than ten International trap fields on our continent.

In recognition of this problem, in 1962 the ATA began registering Modified Clay Pigeon targets, using a modification developed by the National Rifle Association of the standard American trap field and a single trap. Hopefully, in time a growing familiarity with NRA Modified Clay Pigeon shooting will help to develop in our country a group of trapshooters who can cope successfully with International conditions, but we have a long way to go to prove to the rest of the world that we, the greatest shotgun shooting nation of any, can really win at the International game.

Fine individual achievements like Tom Garrigus' Silver medal in the 1968 Olympics and Kenneth Jones' 1966 World Championship are likely to remain isolated phenomena unless we as a country can find a way to provide training and competitive opportunities under International conditions for our young shooters. If we can succeed in that, we can count on them to provide the dedication, but without the physical opportunity, no amount of dedication can get the job done. So if you ever get where you think the regulation ATA game we've been dealing with is not enough of a challenge for you, great— take a look across the pond and see if you can't find enough challenge in the way they play the game there.

Well, there you have it—everything I know how to put down on paper that might help you to shoot trap more skillfully, more successfully and with greater satis-

Various ways in which existing facilities can be adapted for NRA Modified Clay Pigeon shooting and (overleaf) regulation 15-trap International Trap. The United States needs more of these facilities, especially the regulation layout, if we are to show the rest of the world the kind of shotgun shooting we're capable of.

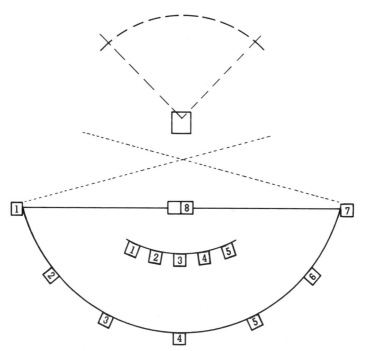

Diagram of skeet field with NRA Modified Clay Pigeon. Regulation ATA trap house used with Modified trap machine.

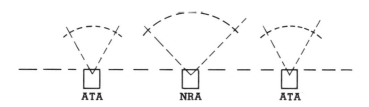

NRA Modified Clay Pigeon between regulation trap fields.

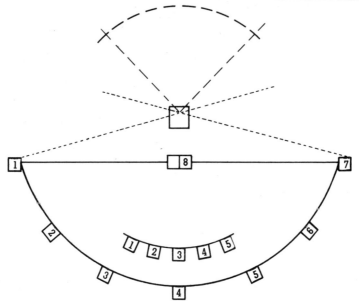

Diagram of skeet field with NRA Modified Clay Pigeon. Modified trap house is centered under skeet target's crossing point.

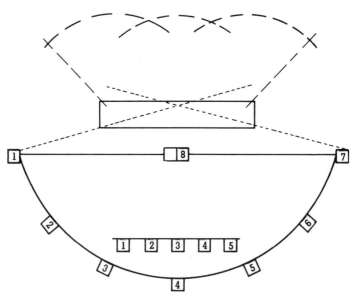

Diagram of skeet field with Clay Pigeon (15 trap). Center trap machine located under skeet target's crossing point.

faction. If it doesn't come to you all at once, don't despair —keep telling yourself that top shooters are made, not born, and every top shooter once had to go through the same slow learning process. They all had to walk before they could run. You can do what they did, only better. It just takes concentration, gun fit and enough practice to give you a complete command over the fundamentals. Perfect these things, and you will come out a winner. Of course, "the sun doesn't shine on the same dog's tail every day." But I'll bet that if you follow my advice, yours will get a lot more sun than the other fellow's!

Picture Credits

The author wishes to thank *Trap & Field* for permission to reproduce the photographs appearing on pages 32-33, 142 and 150-151, and the Winchester-Western Division of Olin Corporation for the pictures on pages 38, 50, 55, 57, 58, 113, 123, 145 and 155. All other photographs were taken by Nick Karas. The line diagrams were executed by George H. Buehler.

Score Better
at Skeet

*To my lovely wife, Peggy,
for her understanding, advice,
and patience while
this book was being written.*

A Word To Left-Handed Shooters and Mss.

Skeet is just as good a game for left-handers as it is for right-handers, and it's just as much fun for the "hers" as for the "hims." However, the following pages mostly call the shooter "him" and assume that he's right-handed, simply because the majority is that way, and it makes instruction writing so much less complicated. And frankly, I suspect that the girl shooters have already solved very well the problems of living in a man's world, just as most left-handers have become adept at making their own translations from the right-handed.

CONTENTS

INTRODUCTION

Skeet is a marvelous game. Designed originally to improve field shooting, it has long since developed into a fascinating sport in its own right, a sociable yet demanding pastime which can be played by young and old alike, of either sex, on any level from a casual tune-up for the hunting season to the concentrated pressure of the world championship.

Collectively, skeet shooters make up a world of their own, a world in which I've experienced some of the proudest moments of my life, and frankly, some of the most humbling ones, too. If you're already a skeet shooter, you know what I mean. If you're not, let me urge you to join the clan and share the fun. I don't think you'll regret it.

How do you become a good shot? Ideally, how to shoot, like many other things, should be handed down from father to son. It might have happened to me that way, for Dad was a great shot. Some of my fondest memories are of riding on the bird wagon with him when I was only ten and watching him drop two or three quail out of every covey rise with his old Winchester pump gun. I've seen him triple on green-winged teal, and that takes some shooting.

Sadly, a fatal car accident robbed me of the chance to learn the secrets of Dad's shooting skill directly from him, and it wasn't until I'd taken up skeet and was shooting every day that I ever came close to filling his hunting boots. It had taken me ten years to learn things he could have explained to me in ten minutes.

Yes, Dad could have taught me a lot. But even he couldn't have made me into a good shot overnight; surely much of his ability with a shotgun, like much of mine, derived from nothing fancier than lots of practice. Dad used to hunt four afternoons a week—five, if he could sneak away after church on Sunday—and he pointed a gun as naturally as pointing a finger. Dad was a great believer in practice. "Take any old bird dog," he liked to say, "and hunt him enough and kill enough birds over him, and you can make him a champion."

Nobody can do your practicing for you—you've got to run up your own mileage. But it sure does help if someone can show you the right things to practice, so that you develop good habits instead of perfecting bad ones. And it also helps if someone can spot your problem when you start going bad. I should know, for I've spent the best part of my life as a tournament shooter and teacher, spotting my own mistakes and others', and I've had a lot of opportunities to observe how tough it can be to straighten yourself out or help someone if you don't know where to look.

In this book I've tried to share my knowledge with you—not only the knowledge of how to break skeet targets, but also the reasons why you miss.

If you're a AAA shooter, AA or even A, you don't need any advice from me. But if you're a B, there's still room for improvement, and perhaps I can show you some little wrinkle that will put you up with the big boys. And if you're plodding along in C or D, I just *know* I can help you, right away.

If this book can help you to jump a class or two, break a few more targets, break 'em cleaner, or enjoy breaking them more, then all my efforts will have been worthwhile. And if we meet on the skeet field some day and you want help, don't hesitate to ask. I am not above doing the same thing myself.

Fred Missildine

Sea Island, Georgia
March 1, 1972

1

HOW
IT ALL STARTED

SKEET shooting is only a baby as target games go, hardly half a century old and thus well over a hundred years the junior of trap shooting. The family is an old one, however, for target sports as a group probably date farther back than any other competitive activities except foot racing and girl chasing (which amount to the same thing). Once primitive man heaved his first rock at an object, it wasn't long before he was getting together with his cavemates to see who could come closest to the aiming mark. And shortly thereafter, no doubt, someone was standing at his shoulder telling him what he was doing wrong. This progressed right on through the spear, bow and arrow, blunderbuss, Kentucky rifle, and finally into the shotgun stage.

Unlike those sports whose origins were strictly recreational, skeet shooting came about as a direct response to a practical need. Until the beginning of the twentieth century, wild game produced an apparently inexhaustible supply of targets for the shotgunner, and it was not until the more or less sudden demise of the passenger pigeon that hunters began to recognize the need for game conservation in the modern sense. But even before World War I, the average hunter was finding that short seasons and small bag limits were making it almost impossible to get enough practice to become a good shot. Too often he found himself driving a long way to hunt, spending a lot of money, and then missing most of his shots and feeling pretty darn foolish. Some shooters turned to trap shooting for pre-season practice, only to find that it did not really help their field shooting that much because of the absence of true crossing shots and incomers.

This was the problem to which a certain Charles E. Davies of Andover, Massachusetts, addressed himself. Davies was the owner of the Glen Rock Kennels and a thoroughly dedicated upland shooter. He was also a man who took his misses seriously, and if he missed the same shot twice in a row, he was prepared to find out why and to do something about it. He used to get his son, Henry, and a friend of Henry's named William Harnden Foster to take a pair of hand traps out into the field and throw clays that simulated his problem shot until he'd licked it. Of course, Henry and Bill Foster had a go at the problem shots too, and before long they all got their heads together to develop a shooting game that provided practice at the whole range of shots the upland shooter might encounter.

After trying and discarding many plans, they finally decided that the one closest to what they were looking for would be a field laid out in a 50-yard circle (later reduced to 40). Around the circle they had twelve stations. A single trap, which was located at Station 12, fired clay targets toward Station 6, and the game was informally called "shooting around the clock." Each

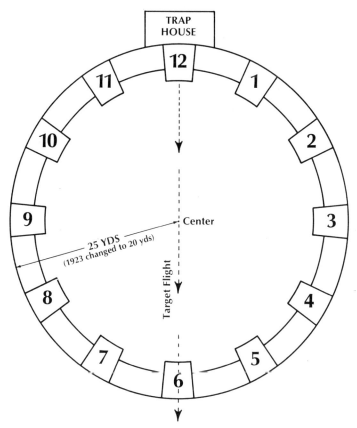

Original "Around the Clock" shooting game, before the clock was halved and its radius reduced to 20 yards.

shooter fired twice from every position, and the 25th shot in the box of shells was taken as a stunt shot from the center of the circle. This layout provided every type of shot a shooter could expect to find while hunting in the field. Even the center shot, which was straight overhead, gave such an excellent challenge to snap shooting that it was soon taken very seriously.

All went well, and before long Davies' game attracted other local shooters. But then one day the man who

owned the adjoining property began complaining that
shot from half of the clock was trespassing on his property. Nothing daunted, Davies cut the field in half with
his back to his neighbor's house, put the trap on Station
6, and added a second trap at Station 12. Instead of
the 12 stations, he now had seven on the remaining half
circle, plus the old center station as an eighth. After a
while, he raised one of the houses to add variety.

That was the beginning of modern skeet, though at
the time, the game wasn't called "skeet." It was just a
game to improve field shooting. The high house simulated a duck coming into the decoys. The low house, on
the other hand, simulated a rising target of an upland
game such as grouse or pheasant. By walking around
the half-circle the shooter got every shot from a straightaway at Station 1 to a right-angle crossing shot at Station 4. The targets came out anywhere with a delay of
one to three seconds, giving the unknown timing with
which live game breaks from cover. Also, the shooter
was required to keep the gun at a ready position with
the butt showing below the elbow to simulate walking
in the field. Doubles were added at Stations 1, 2, 6,
and 7. This gave the sensation of shooting a double in
the field, or a left and right as it's known today.

Most shooters used the same gun they used in the
bird field during the hunting season. Thus a week or
two before the season opened a shooter could go out to
the skeet field and shoot a few rounds, so that when
the time came to go hunting, he could pick up his gun
and have it feel like an old friend instead of a club. By
getting this early practice the shooter found himself
way ahead of the game when the season opened.

The game grew in popularity. Not only did it lack
the seriousness of trap shooting, but it took longer to
complete the circle around the field. More and more
shooters came to the club to shoot. Naturally, competi-

tion sprang up. It was time to begin to formalize the game and develop rules that would be the same for all.

Most of the promotion and publicity that helped launch the game was the result of Foster's efforts. In 1920 he became assistant editor of the *National Sportsman*, a magazine that had a big following. As the game evolved he began to publish articles about it, and most of the subsequent refinements in its development are attributable to him.

In 1926, Foster prepared a well-rounded program for shooting the game and even rules for inter-club competitions. He kicked it off in the February issues of *National Sportsman* and *Hunting and Fishing*, a sister magazine. As an added boost, he decided to turn to the public to seek a new name for the game and offered a $100 prize for the best suggestion. Gertrude Hurlbutt of Dayton, Montana, came up with the winner, an old Scandinavian word meaning "to shoot", and *skeet* became the accepted word for "shooting around the clock" (or half-clock, as it had now become).

The year 1926 was a milestone for skeet in more than one way. That year, the Raleigh Skeet Club of North Carolina won what was termed the first National Skeet Shooting Championship. It was also in that first year that anyone ever went straight in the new game. (This distinction is credited to H. M. Jackson, Jr., of Garner, North Carolina.) By the end of the year, a National Skeet Shooting Association had formed, precursor of the organization that today sanctions skeet tournaments throughout the United States and Canada.

In the formulative years of skeet, much of the impetus for the game came from the *National Sportsman*. The magazine acted as sponsor and financially supported the group for several decades. But because of this direct support, other magazines in the field seemed to shun the game and its coverage. In 1946, the publishers

A notable site: Remington's famed Lordship, Conn. skeet layout, home of the Great Eastern, as it looked a couple of decades ago. The expanse in the background is Long Island Sound, which has been known to serve up some pretty tricky winds on occasion.

of the magazine decided, for the good of the sport, to sever their relationship and give up their sponsorship of the National Skeet Shooting Association. On October 23, the organization was dissolved and then reorganized immediately under a new board of directors. It assumed the old name but adopted a new charter. Incorporation took place under the laws of the state of Delaware and headquarters were established in Dallas, Texas, where they remain today.

THE MODERN GAME

Skeet as we know it today has changed very little since the days when Davies and Foster changed "shooting around the clock" to shooting only *halfway* around the clock in the mid-1920s. The changes that have occurred are relatively subtle. The field remains substantially the same, but the target's angle of flight has been shifted slightly in the interest of safety. When Foster originally cut the clock in half, all targets flew directly over Station 8 and the opposite house. As the demand for more fields grew, the target crossing point was moved 18 feet out in front of Station 8. This made it possible to place fields side by side, utilizing a common trap house in the center, and added a great deal more safety.

The target remains the same, but the distance has been increased to 60 yards, giving the shooter a slightly tougher target to shoot. The three-second delay has long since been abandoned, mostly due to the difficulty of producing satisfactory equipment. The rule requiring the shooter to keep the gun dismounted from the shoulder when calling for the target has also been rescinded. This was changed for the simple reason that it proved a very difficult rule for referees to apply consistently; many infractions were ignored, and a lot of hard feelings resulted. Now the shooter can call for the bird with his gun mounted or dismounted, as he prefers. Both of these changes were made in the interest of making the application of rules as fair as possible for all competitors, and keeping the game moving. I'm not sure that they were right, but the game has caught on, and it's hard to argue with success. The international form of the game never changed either of these rules, and participants in the Olympic Games and World Championships still shoot with a low gun and a one- to three-second delay. International skeet is discussed in more detail in the last chapter of this book.

Although this book is written primarily for the experienced shooter, it's quite possible that someone will read it who doesn't understand modern skeet at all. So, if you hotshots will take five, I'll take five and recap the game as it is shot today.

A round of skeet consists of 25 targets. Sixteen of them are single shots from each trap house at Stations 1 through 8. At Stations 1, 2, 6 and 7, two targets are thrown at the same time and referred to as doubles. The four pair added to the 16 single targets makes 24. Until 1971, the 25th target was called the optional, for if the shooter had broken all his targets until then, he could pick any station he wished for his final shot. (Generally, the choice was Low 7 or High 7.) If the shooter misses any earlier target, however, his optional is an immediate repeat of his first miss. The normal form of skeet called for a five-man squad to shoot all its singles targets first, and then return to Stations 1, 2, 6, and 7 for the doubles, and some clubs still follow this routine as standard.

Today, however, the so-called "speed-up" system has become the standard for all of skeet shooting as well as tournaments. In speed-up skeet, the double at Stations 1, 2, 6, and 7 is shot immediately after the singles, and if the shooter runs his first 24 birds straight, he *must* shoot Low 8 again as his last target. I don't like this system quite as well as the old way, but it does save a lot of time, and frankly, I think it's easier on the shooter.

Today the rules call for the target to fly a minimum distance of 60 yards, and the end of the flight must be marked by a stake. The distance from Station 1 to the target crossing point is 21 yards. The high house target begins its flight 10 feet above the ground and crosses the target point 15 feet above the level at Station 8. The low house bird leaves the chute 3½ feet above ground level and travels over the same crossing point stake, at the same height, as the high house target. Targets may be thrown more than 60 yards but not over 70. This distance is always measured in still air, usually early in the morning, before the wind comes. During a tournament, once the traps are set they are very seldom changed.

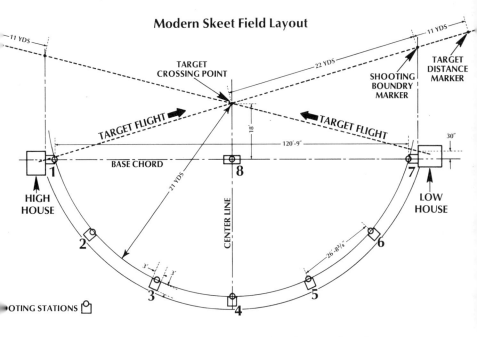

Modern Skeet Field Layout

Distance between shooting stake and trap house is three feet.

Today, the game that Davies and Foster originated and developed for the benefit of a half-dozen hunters, in order to improve their field shooting, has grown into a sport played at more than 700 clubs by over 18,000 registered and innumerable unregistered shooters, many of whom have no interest in hunting at all. Despite the

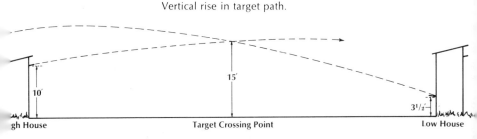

Vertical rise in target path.

Skeet fields as far as the eye can see: a general view of only some of the fields at the Texas International Gun Club in San Antonio, site of the 1971 World Skeet Championships.

Skeet shooting is every bit as good a game for women as for men. Not only do they break their targets just as cleanly, they sure do improve the scenery, as this Lordship squad demonstrates.

pressure on hunting and shooting activities generally, it is still a fast-growing recreational activity, for it has many advantages—it is one of the few sports in which one can practice and compete at the same time, and one of the few sports that the whole family can play together, from youth to quite an advanced age. (It's a sport that even paraplegics can play, for that matter, and some of them shoot very well.) I think it's a great game, and I'm glad Davies and Foster thought it up.

Now that all the preliminaries are out of the way, let's get down to business and figure out why you haven't broken your last 100 straight.

2

SKEET GUNS AND EQUIPMENT

THE game itself hasn't changed much, but skeet guns and equipment have changed a heap since the days of Davies and Foster. Around World War I, most skeet shooters showed up in their old canvas hunting coat or vest and shot their favorite upland game gun. If they didn't have a short-barrel gun, they shot what they had. Any old gun would do. In fact, young Dick Shaughnessy won his first National Championship in 1936 with a 16-gauge side-by-side double gun. Today you would be lucky to find a half-dozen side-by-sides among the seven or eight hundred shooters attending the National or World's Championship, as it is called today.

Times change and so does equipment. You probably have your favorite skeet gun already picked out and locked away in a safe place until your next tournament. However, it never hurts to look at what the other fellow is using, especially if he's beating you to death with it.

So let's take a look at what's being used today to break all of the old records and set new ones.

CHOICE OF ACTION

Skeet guns must be capable of firing two shots. So this narrows the actions down to the autoloader, over-and-under, pump gun, and the double-barrel side-by-side. Their popularity is in the same order, with the autoloader an overwhelming favorite. It has a number of advantages—it doesn't have to be pumped on doubles,

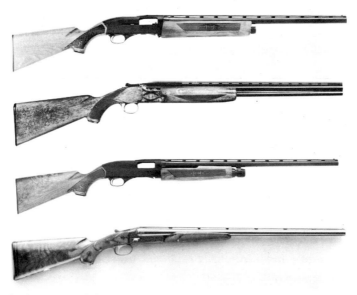

The four types of skeet-gun actions, in descending order of popularity today: Top, the autoloader, second, the over-and-under, third, the pump or slide-action, and bottom, the side-by-side double gun. (The guns are all Winchesters, Models 1400, 101, 1200 and 21 respectively.) Ventilated ribs are standard on the skeet gun, along with center and front bead sights; recoil pads are not, though many shooters add them.

absorbs most of the recoil in the course of operating the action, can be obtained in the same model in all four gauges, and it doesn't cost an arm and a leg to buy one.

The last two considerations are important ones if you take your skeet seriously. It is a big advantage to shoot the same model gun in all four gauges. Switching from one gun to another is tough enough, switching from one model to another somewhat tougher, and switching from one type of action to another almost impossible.

If you are addicted to the snappy handling qualities of the over-and-under, can handle the recoil, and have a rich uncle, you may well be satisfied with a matched set of double guns, or a set of interchangeable barrels or tubes. Any of these alternatives will set you back considerably more than the set of four autoloaders, but that's your problem. I can't tell you which action to use, for guns are like friends—everyone has to choose his own. Just because I shoot four Winchester pumps, and the best shot at your club shoots Krieghoffs, doesn't mean that either one would suit you. In this game of skeet it's all up to you and the gun, so try them all and then do your own thing. Find out what suits you best, and stick to it. It took me three years of experimenting before I finally found that I shot the pump actions best. Operating that old corn-shucker seems to keep my timing smooth.

However, if you are a novice shooter, or a lightweight—lady, junior, or person of slight stature—I'll be less equivocal and give you some positive, sound advice: get an autoloader. I'd start with a 20-gauge. At the beginning you'll hit as many targets with it as you would with a 12. The 20-gauge has very little recoil, and enough weight to keep your swing going smoothly. And when you're learning to shoot, recoil is a very important thing. Lots of shooters claim they never feel it, but the fact remains, it's there; and the novice can very easily bruise himself enough at first to take all the fun out of shooting. He is particularly vulnerable to this in doubles.

There's an old expression that, "a mule can't pull if he's kicking," and so it is with your gun. If you and your gun are not working together, the results are not going to be what you expect. Let me put it this way: You're in this game for one reason and that's to break targets. Don't let anything sway your decision. Find the type of action that gives you the most pleasure when you shoot it. Get it fitted correctly, as described in the next chapter, and then go to work on your position and concentration. Mount it right, stand right, tell it to do the right thing, and it will break the target every time.

BARREL LENGTH

Barrel length doesn't need much discussion. All standard skeet guns come with 26-inch barrels. This is as it should be, as skeet is a fast-swinging game. Although a longer barrel would narrow the apparent lead required, it takes too long to start it swinging.

Some shooters maintain that due to the difference in receiver lengths, over-and-unders and side-by-side guns need a 28-inch barrel to make them as long as a 26-inch pump gun or autoloader. This is true. But, after trying every make of double gun in both barrel lengths, I still find that the 26-inch barrel is faster, balances better and does a better job. For every shooter in the record book who uses a 28-inch barrel there are twenty who do not.

I use a 26-inch barrel on all my pump guns, and recommend it for everyone except king-size shooters. If you're taller than 6'3", a 28-inch barrel may feel more comfortable and provide better balance. Otherwise, stick with the shorties.

CHOKE

As with barrel length, there's not much to say when it comes to the best pattern for breaking skeet targets. All shots are comparatively close, and at about the same distance except for Station 8, which is even closer. Most targets are broken just before, or just past, the target crossing point—the average distance is approximately 21 yards from the shooter. The choke that patterns best at this distance is an open improved-cyclinder, which we call a "skeet" choke.

Obviously, a regular full-choke barrel patterning 70 percent at 40 yards would be like shooting a rifle at 21 yards. You'd pulverize what you hit, but you'd waste an awful lot of lead on the sky. The wider you can open up your barrel *and still keep the pattern even*, the better off you'll be. Full-cylinder barrels with no choke constriction at all (such as a 30-incher that's been sawed off to 26 inches) throw big patterns, but they're often splotched with holes you could throw a cat through, not to mention a clay target. The good skeet barrel always has at least a couple of thousandths of an inch of constriction.

Pattern your barrel at 21 yards, not at 40. What difference does it make how the average works out at a distance you're never going to shoot the gun at? I'd look for a barrel that puts about 70 percent of a big, even pattern into a 30-inch circle at 21 yards. That ought to do the job on the bird if you do yours, and still leave you some leeway.

At one time double guns and over-and-unders were bored improved-cylinder in one barrel and about modified-cylinder in the other. This was known as Skeet 1

and Skeet 2. These skeet designations are being phased
out today by most manufacturers, partly because the
overwhelming number of guns they produce are single-
barrelled, and also because the modified-cylinder which
was usually fired on the second target proved to be too
tight for this type of shot.

Anyhow, before you decide to change your choke or
buy a new barrel with a different choke, pattern your
shotgun. Beginning shooters seldom if ever pattern their
guns, and experienced shooters aren't much better.
There's an old belief that once you pattern your gun
you'll want to change it, or lose confidence in it. This
is just simply an old wives' tale. Why rely completely
on the choke stamped by the manufacturer on the barrel,
which may or may not have some relationship to reality?
Take the time to check it out yourself, and you may be
surprised. Know your pattern and know your gun.
You'll have more confidence than ever before.

SKEET LOADS

The skeet shells that we fire today are the finest ever
produced. Over a million are fired in the factories for
quality control alone. Most of the improvements now
used in the standard field loads were created for, and
tested at, the skeet field. Skeet load requirements
are set by the National Skeet Shooting Association simply to give everyone the same chance while participating
in tournaments.

Shot sizes may be number 9 or larger. But unlike
field shooting, in which large shot is sometimes necessary to make a clean kill, skeet targets are rotating
so fast that centrifugal force alone will cause a target
to break if it is hit by only one or two small pellets.
By using the smallest permissible shot, it is possible
to get more shot into the 1⅛-ounce shot load. The more

shot, the more chances of hitting the target, therefore, the more breaks.

Let me pass on something that I learned while trap shooting. The 12-gauge shell is made in two loads. Both carry 1⅛ ounces of shot, but one has 2¾ drams equivalent of powder while the other has 3 drams. The 2¾-dram load will get the job done just as well, if not better, than the 3-dram load and has only half the recoil. The less recoil, the better the concentration. If you have not tried this load, I strongly suggest that you do so. Most good shooters have already changed to it.

SIGHTS AND BEADS

Shotguns are built to use on moving targets, to be pointed and not aimed. If they are pointed, there's little need for a rear sight, and without a rear sight, the front sight is useless. Let me put it this way: The front end of the barrel is the front sight, your eye is the rear sight. Get the two lined up and the point of impact of the shot charge will be exactly where you are looking.

The primary function of the bead on the front of the gun is simply to give you a reference point. The middle bead, halfway down the rib, helps prevent canting the gun. A small ivory or red bead is all that is necessary. Stay away from large beads; they only distract your attention from the target. If possible, carry a couple of spare beads with you. Unimportant as they are, it is still distracting to knock one off during a shoot. (I did this in Jacksonville, years ago, and wound up with an 89 X 100 in the 12-gauge event. I was so mad and disgusted that as soon as I returned home the next day, I shot four rounds with the same gun—no bead—and broke 100 straight, proving how easy it is to make a mountain out of a molehill.)

RIBS

All skeet guns should be equipped with a ventilated rib. If yours does not have one and you are not an AAA shooter, then I suggest that you get one. You can do this simply by sending the gun to Simmon's Gun Specialties or another good gunsmith. A good rib is a great help. It not only makes cross-firing almost impossible, it also prevents the heat waves rising from the barrel from distorting your vision. On some guns it adds just enough weight to the front end of the gun to give good balance.

Nowadays there are several types of ventilated ribs. They are all good. I suggest that you send your gun to Simmon's and let him put on what he knows is best for your gun. It is worth every nickle that you pay for it.

RECOIL PADS

We have talked about every other part of the gun, so let me add my two cents on recoil pads. I don't like them. Maybe I've seen too many that were put on wrong. Then, too, I am a drop stock shooter, never mounting the gun until after I have seen the target, and a recoil pad tends to stop the gun from sliding smoothly into place in the shoulder pocket.

I believe that if a gun is fitted correctly, especially one of the new autoloaders, there is little need for a recoil pad. However, there are exceptions to every rule. If you shoot with a mounted gun, you may find that a recoil pad helps prevent the stock from sliding off your shoulder, especially on the double shots. Or if you shoot one of the over-and-unders, it may help reduce the recoil.

If you get a recoil pad, get one of the ventilated types, for they have much more shock-absorbing ability.

Secondly, be sure to keep the same length of pull and downpitch on your stock when you add the pad. Too many so-called gunsmiths simply add the recoil pad to your stock, changing the length of pull, or cut the stock at the wrong angle, changing the downpitch. Make sure it's installed right. I've never used any of the recoil reducers that are imbedded in the stock. I suppose they're all right if you still like the gun balance after installation.

GLASSES

Now that we have discussed the gun, let's review the other equipment you'll need before going on to the actual shooting. The first is glasses. These are a must in skeet shooting, for safety if for no other reason.

What the well-equipped skeet shooter will wear: Glasses, ear-plugs, practical headgear and a good vest. The left-hand glove is strictly optional, but shooters who perspire freely find that it helps. This shooter's left-hand position is also strictly optional—a position much further back on the fore-end suits most shooters much better—but he sure knows how to check the stock correctly.

Don't hand me the stuff that you can't shoot with glasses. You wouldn't think of driving down the road at 60 miles an hour on slick tires would you? Then why stand there and try to break a target coming almost directly at you at 60 miles an hour, any piece of which could put out an eye. I'm not trying to scare you—well, maybe I am, at that. Next time when you are at Low 7, take a look at the trap house. If a target can do that to the trap house, think of what it can do to you.

If you are a serious skeet shooter, you should have two pairs of shooting glasses, not only for safety but to help you cope with the changing light conditions, which can very noticeably affect how well you see or do not see the targets. On bright, sunny days you need normal green or gray glasses. They shouldn't be too dark, but dark enough to keep you from squinting. The lenses should be large enough to keep you from seeing the rims. On overcast days or on days when you find yourself shooting late in the afternoon, switch to either clear or yellow-tinted glasses. A good yellow lens has a helpful light-gathering quality.

Here's another tip: always put your glasses on at least fifteen minutes before you go out to shoot. This gives your eyes a chance to get used to the change in light conditions. If you are in a shoot-off, keep your clear or yellow-tinted glasses handy. Very often shoot-offs wind up in the late, late afternoon. A man who keeps his dark glasses on after the sun goes down is shooting at a distinct disadvantage. Change to your clear glasses if you have prescriptions. The better you see, the better you hit the targets.

EAR PLUGS

There are a number of ear plugs on the market today, ranging all the way from the simple plug-in type to the expensive custom-fitted jobs. Some shooters still use cotton.

Doctors seem to think that while all deaf people are not skeet shooters, all skeet shooters go deaf. I have to disagree with them. There is a small percentage of people who really are bothered by the noise. These extra-sensitive people should wear both plugs and ear muffs, to prevent hearing damage. The rest of the shooters can shoot with little if any ill effect to their hearing, *provided that they take normal precautions.* Ear plugs are like life boats on a steamer. You may not need them, but it doesn't hurt to have them. I not only recommend that children use ear plugs, but I insist on it. See that you do the same if you have a youngster starting to shoot. And don't take his word for it. Every now and then lift his hair just to be sure that he's got them in his ears! A few die-hards claim that ear plugs disrupt their shooting. Be sure to speak up, when you tell them how wrong they are!

CLOTHING

Clothing is the last of our physical factors, but it could well be the most important of the three. As we've said, skeet shooters once liked to wear their field clothing to the ranges. Today, however, shooting and styles have changed greatly. Above all, your shooting clothing should be comfortable, allowing freedom of movement. The shoulder patch should be soft and pliable, and not too thick. I've seen many shooting coats and vests that had a pad at least a quarter-inch thick. Skeet clothing should never be bulky, even if you need warmth. If you shoot in cold climates, you can get warmth without bulk by using several layers of thin clothing instead of one heavy layer. The nylon wind shirts often worn by skiers over a turtle neck pullover and a thermal undershirt are about all I've ever needed. In late-afternoon shooting, when it is likely to cool a bit, I slip on a nylon golf jacket, then put my shooting vest over this.

What you wear on your feet is also quite important. Shoes should be relatively sturdy for comfort and support and come equipped with rubber or composition ground-gripping soles for steadiness. Ladies should never shoot in high heels.

Gloves are not necessary unless the weather is really cold. However, there is something of a trend today toward wearing gloves. Shooters whose palms sweat under tension find that they benefit from them. I recommend that if you don't need them, don't wear them. There's nothing like the feel of your own finger on the trigger when it comes time to pull it.

Once you have selected your clothing, stick with it, shoes and all. What you become accustomed to will allow you to concentrate more and more on the target.

3

GUN FIT

WHEN it comes to buying a new suit or pair of shoes, most people are pretty fussy. They want the style, color, and fit to be perfect. I've heard guys raise a fair commotion on how soft their eggs should be boiled, and how dry their martinis should be mixed. But strangely, some of these same individuals will go into a gun shop and spend a month's salary for a shotgun without giving the slightest thought to whether or not it fits them.

It's true, of course, that many gun salesmen aren't much help. In fact, getting a gun fitted properly is like buying a cold beer in Georgia on Sunday—not too difficult if you know where to go, but an awful waste of time otherwise. The average hardware store gun salesman is happier selling lawn mowers, and he figures you ought to be able to wrap yourself around any factory stock well enough, as long as your credit is good. And in a way, he's right. The factory skeet stock does fit a lot of shooters. And even those it doesn't fit are perfectly capable of shooting good scores with it.

In this respect, skeet is different from trap or field shooting, where 90 percent of the shots are made at unknown angles, and the fit of the gun takes precedence over everything else. But in skeet shooting the flight of the target is known and it is possible, *by taking the correct position*, to overcome a poorly fitted gun and break AA scores.

Then why bother about correct gun fit? Let me put the answer this way—shooting a gun that does not fit is like wearing a pair of shoes a half-size too small, or driving a car with the seat too far back. You get where you're going, but it's much harder work.

THE IMPORTANCE OF GUN FIT

Breaking the bird depends on where the gun is pointed when you touch it off and how you track the target. But these depend not only on which way you're headed, but also on your shape, the gun's shape, and how they fit together once the gun has been mounted. It is highly desirable that the gun should fit you correctly, for if it doesn't fit, much of the time, effort, and money you put into the improving of your shooting will go right down the drain. Of course, it's just as essential for you to know how to mount the gun correctly, for even a perfectly fitted gun cannot help you if you put the gun in the wrong spot. I'll give you a complete run-down on this in the next chapter. For now, I just want you to understand that having a correctly fitted gun accomplishes three main things: First, it insures that the gun will shoot exactly where you point it. Second, this knowledge lets you transfer most of your concentration to the target; and finally, it holds recoil to a bare minimum.

You'd be amazed at the number of shooters who use guns that don't fit them, but still break good scores. The real question is, however, how much better could they be if their guns were fitted correctly? It seems to me that this problem of poorly fitted guns is getting worse because so many new shooters use the shouldered gun and really can't tell if their gun is fitted properly or not. For when the gun is shouldered before the swing is started, there is ample time to adjust to the stock. If it has too much drop, the shooter simply holds the gun lower on the shoulder, or raises his head until he can see over the gun's receiver. However, if he shoulders his gun only after calling for the target, the crooked stock will let the receiver come up so high that it will blot out the end of the barrel, and the shooter will be punching out O's instead of X's.

Gun fit is important in skeet shooting because of the speed at which the game is played on the one hand, and the length to which it is played—call it "fatigue factor"—on the other. Though the targets are thrown at known angles, the shooter must start swinging on them almost instantly in order to break them. The flight of the bird is so fast that no time can be spent in re-adjusting the gun once it is mounted. There is no time to wrap yourself around the gun and aim as in rifle

B=Length of barrel.
S=Length of stock (Pull).
HH′=Drop at heel of butt.
CC′=Drop at comb.

TH′=Length stock at heel } determine pitch
TT′=Length stock at toe }

GUN MEASUREMENT

shooting. There is only time to look. The gun must point where you look, automatically, if you are to break targets consistently. If you have to bend yourself three ways until Sunday in order to get down on the gun, when you get into a long shoot-off you'll find fatigue taking over. You are not only apt to miss the hard targets, but you will find yourself missing the easy targets like High 1 and Low 7, targets you ought to be counting on for a little rest.

Most American manufacturers stock their skeet guns to about the following dimensions:

Length of pull...................14 inches
Drop at heel...................2½ inches
Drop at comb..................1½ inches
Pitch down ....2 inches

In practice, about three shooters out of four can accommodate themselves quite nicely to stocks of these dimensions. However, if you're much on the tall, short, thin, or fat side of "average," you're going to need help.

Where can you get it? A few of the better gun shops have what is known as a try-gun, a shotgun with a hinged skeleton stock that can be adjusted for every dimension. If you know where there is a try-gun and fitter who knows how to use it, consider yourself lucky. Qualified gun fitters are as rare as four-leaf clovers. Alternatively, try to get help from a professional shooting coach, or one of the topnotch shooters who is an "industry representative." If you are lucky enough to find a really qualified fitter, take his advice, whether or not you like it at first.

A gun that really fits you is a pleasure to shoot, and this itself is a factor in scoring. After all, scores are mostly a matter of concentration, and concentration comes from confidence—not only confidence in yourself, but also in your gun and the knowledge that it

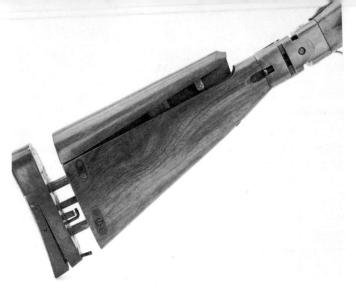

The try-gun stock, adjustable for length of pull, pitch, drop at comb and heel, and even cast-off.

fits you. The fraction-of-an-inch difference in gun fit between something approximate and something just right can be the difference between a 99 and a 100, or between a bird in the pot and just feathers.

Let's suppose that you appreciate how important gun fit is, but have no qualified stockfitter on tap. Here is a short, do-it-yourself program that might put your mind at ease. It was my privilege to learn this from one of the world's finest stock-fitters, Paul Doane, now retired from Winchester-Western. A good many different factors are involved in correct stock fit. Some are more important than others, so let's discuss them in sequence. Of the five principal measurements—pull, drop at comb and at heel, pitch, and cast-off—the length of pull is by far the most important, and also the most abused. So let's start with it.

LENGTH OF PULL

To determine the proper length of the stock, take your gun and assume a natural stance, toes about a foot apart and their tips facing about 45 degrees from the direction of aim. After making sure that the gun is empty and the safety is on, place the butt in the crook of your elbow, the muzzle pointing straight up. You should just be able to reach the trigger with the first joint of your finger. If you can reach the trigger only with the tip of your first finger, the stock is too long and should be shortened. If the finger goes through the trigger guard to the second joint, the stock is too short and should be lengthened.

Now raise the gun naturally to your shoulder, with the thumb around the grip and the first joint of the trigger finger on the trigger. Put your head down to the stock. There should be approximately one inch of clearance between the base of the thumb and your nose.

The quickest way to determine if the length of pull is approximately correct. If you have to stretch to place the first joint of your trigger finger on the trigger, or cannot do so at all, the stock is too long; if you can reach the trigger with the second joint, the stock is too short.

Remember, the stock should be snug in the shoulder pocket (the slight depression between the collar bone and the knob of the shoulder joint) and not on the bicep. If your nose winds up against the base of your thumb or within a half-inch of it, your stock is too short. On the other hand, if your face is well back on the stock, more than an inch, the stock is too long.

It's possible for a shooter to become a champion while shooting a gun too short for him, but I've never seen one who was shooting a gun that was too long. This is due to the fact that on quartering or hard-angling shots, the long stock will bind and kill your swing, and your head will come off the gun. Too short a stock will permit you to bust the target, but you'll also bust your own nose with the base of your thumb.

Length of pull, of all the stock dimensions, is the easiest one to change. You simply add spacers onto the stock or remove some wood. Once it's right, leave it alone. If you miss targets, look in the mirror. It's your fault and not in the gun.

Unless you are a midget, never shorten a stock to less than 13 inches. If you do, it will concentrate too much recoil in too small an area. All you'll get is a sore shoulder. And let me add a final word of warning. A change of one-quarter or three-eighths of an inch sounds like very little and looks like even less. But I can assure you, it will *feel* like a tremendous amount. So, when you cut or add onto your gun, do it in small segments, and don't chop off an inch or add on an inch all at once. Add on or take off a little at a time until you have it right. Then give it a good try. Don't start hacking again after just a round or two. Remember, new shoes don't feel just right either, the first time you put them on. It takes a little time to break them in and get accustomed to them. It's the same with your gun.

Before we leave the subject of pull, let me add a

Correct stock position with the gun mounted. The stock is snugly in the shoulder pocket, heel just below the top of the shoulder, so that the cheek can rest against the comb without bending the neck or inclining the head too much. The nose is approximately one inch from the base of the right thumb, and the receiver is exactly in line with the right eye.

Incorrect stock position: the butt is too low on the shoulder, a common fault with experienced shooters, and one that requires the head to be bent down too much to obtain the correct sight picture. In practice, the stock is not firmly cheeked, resulting in a false target picture and shooting over the target.

Another incorrect stock position, common with new shooters: the butt is on the bicep, and not in the shoulder pocket. Too long a stock can also produce this position, which results in a bruised arm and shoulder. Note how the head must be canted in order to reach the comb.

Too high a stock position is a common fault with women, junior and slight shooters at first; they lean back to help raise the heavy gun, and end up with their head too far back on the comb for the proper sight picture. It is almost impossible to stay under the target with the gun mounted like this.

few words on trigger fingers. When you check the length of pull, you contact the trigger with the first joint of the first finger, and not the fleshy tip. And of course, you do the same thing when you're shooting. This small detail is of considerable importance, for the fleshy pad of your fingertip has enough "give" in it to affect your timing. Accordingly, you should contact the trigger not with the fleshy pad, but with the crease between the tip and the second segment. There is no give here, for there is no fatty tissue.

It takes only the tiniest fraction of a second to compress fatty tissue, but it is enough to give you a genuine lag, and even worse, a slight sensation of delay. This slight hesitation or pause feels a bit "flinchy," and can actually bring on flinching. So be sure you always pull with the crease and keep your timing constant.

DROP AT HEEL

Just how important is drop at the heel or comb of a shotgun? Well, it's about like having a rich uncle. You can get along without him, but it would sure make things a lot easier if you could get along with him.

I used to hunt quail with a doctor who shot a fine English side-by-side that had been given to him by his wife on their anniversary. Such imported guns are usually stocked very straight. Doc wasn't the best of shots but what bugged him even more is that he missed even the easy straightaways.

One day, Doc pushed an old sow with little ones too far, and she charged him. Since my friend's gun was unloaded, there wasn't much he could do but bop her on the side of her head with the butt of the gun. To his disgust, he cracked the stock, but not badly enough to prevent him from using the gun.

An hour later, after he had killed the next two

straightaways and "wiped my eye" on a hard-angle shot, I finally figured that he had at last "come of age." Not so. When he took the gun in to have the stock repaired, he found that hed bent it down from 2¼ inches to 2½ inches. As you can see, that quarter inch really does make a difference. Before this happened, no matter how hard he had cheeked the gun, he still shot over everything because the stock was too straight for him.

Now, before you go out and wallop the first pig you come to with your favorite skeet gun, let's check it for drop at the heel. With the butt of the stock well in the shoulder pocket and not out on the arm, the heel of the stock should lie well up the shoulder, but not above it. Just about a quarter-inch below would be perfect in my book.

Seldom if ever should skeet or hunting guns need stocks straighter than two inches or with more drop at heel than three inches. The drop at the heel is not as critical as the drop at the comb, so that small differences such as an eighth of an inch are not important enough to warrant change. But a change of a quarter to three-eighths inches up or down is important. If that's the case, see a gunsmith.

DROP AT COMB

Unlike drop at the heel, where small changes of an eighth of an inch make little difference, a change in drop at the comb, no matter how slight, can have a large effect on where your gun is pointed. You might say that drop at the comb is like a ship's barometer— a slight change up or down can make just as much difference in your shooting as a change in the barometer does in the weather.

I would say that drop at the comb was the next most

critical stock dimension to length of pull. For the comb height determines the elevation of your eye in relation to the bore. And, of course, in shotgun shooting your eye is the real rear sight. Therefore, the eye must be positioned for every shot in the same location. It must be centrally placed and only slightly above the rib or receiver groove. In this position, the shooter sees what appears to be a flat, even surface as he looks down the barrel at his target.

If you know how to mount a gun correctly (and if you don't, you'll learn how in the next chapter), there's a pretty good self-test you can make to check the drop at the comb. With the safety on, breech open, and gun unloaded, take the correct stance and mount the gun correctly to the shoulder. Be sure that the gun butt is in the shoulder pocket and not out on the bicep. Then, have someone stand directly in front of you. With your cheek resting on the comb and your nose about one inch from the base of your thumb, point the gun barrel directly at his eye. In this position, he should see the pupil of your eye just as if it were resting on the back of the rib or on the receiver. If there is a good deal of space between the pupil and the rib, more drop at the comb is needed. On the other hand, if the eye is partially or wholly obscured, then somewhat less drop is needed.

If you can't find someone to help you, then do the same thing yourself, but this time close your eyes before you mount the gun. Once you have the gun mounted, cheek on the stock, then open your eyes and look for the groove. The reason you must close your eyes before mounting the gun is that if you leave them open you will compensate and stop the gun where you want it, getting an untrue picture. If you open your eyes and cannot see completely down the rib, then the gun has too much drop and should be straightened. On the other hand, if you are looking up the rib like a staircase, the stock is too straight and the drop at comb, at heel, or both should be increased.

If less drop is needed at the comb, it is very simple to correct. Just add one of the pads sold at the sporting goods stores to the comb. These come in thicknesses of ⅛, ¼, and ⅜ of an inch. If you are unable to get any of these, try adding "moleskin" or plastic friction tape to the comb until the desired height is reached. (Moleskin is a type of felt adhesive sold at all drugstores.)

Adding drop at the comb is quite another story. The only way to do this on most guns is to cut away the comb. As what is cut away cannot be replaced, this can be a costly mistake if not done correctly. If more drop is needed, I suggest that you try to find a gun at your club that has the drop you think you need. Shoot it at least four rounds. If it works, measure the drop at the comb, and have your gunsmith adjust your stock accordingly.

Remember, though, that it's much more common to find shooters using too much drop at comb than too little, and that while it's possible to shoot a gun that is too straight at the comb, it's very difficult to shoot one with too much drop. Changing drop at comb is a major operation; be sure you know what you're doing before making any radical change.

If you shoot all four gauges, all four stocks should be as nearly identical as possible. If you shoot one better than the rest, check its stock dimensions against the other three. Chances are that the comb will be different. And remember, you may be missing the target by only a fraction of an inch, but at the comb and not out where the target is flying.

PITCH

Although pitch is a part of correct gun fit, little need be said about it. Most skeet guns have from 2 to 2½ inches of down pitch. The most practical way to measure pitch is to place a gun against a door jamb with the butt squarely on the sill. The distance from the door jamb to the end of the barrel is the down pitch. If you add a pad to your gun, be careful that you follow the contour of the stock and do not change the down pitch.

It has always been my theory that pitch should only be changed as a matter of comfort. If the toe or heel of the gun is digging into your shoulder and causing a bruise, then the pitch should be changed. Otherwise, leave it alone. In any case, never try to change the point of impact by changing the down pitch of the gun. In fact, the less experimenting you do with pitch, the better off you'll be.

TRIGGER PULL

Technically, trigger pull is also a part of correct gun fit, though it is not something that should be tampered with very much. Most gun manufacturers set their trigger between three and five pounds of pull. Personally, I think this is right for a skeet gun. It is a great mistake to hone your trigger down too fine. Too fine a trigger pull—say, below three pounds—requires so little exertion that it can lead to premature firings. This is especially true when a shooter is swinging hard to catch a bird such as High 2, Low 6, or Station 8. The tendency is for the shooter to pull the trigger with the swing of the gun as he goes after the bird, and often it fires before the bird is actually caught. Also, there is a matter of safety. The trigger that is too fine is apt to go off when the action is closed. Even though this doesn't harm anyone, it can sure upset your concentration, and concentration is the name of the game.

Here again, if you shoot all four guns, they should all have as nearly as possible the same trigger pull. Naturally, if you shoot one gun a great deal more than the other, the trigger pull is going to soften up a bit. So check your other three guns and try to keep them the same as the gun you shoot the most.

Unless you are a darned good amateur gunsmith, any changing of the trigger pull should be done by a qualified repair shop. They will have a trigger pull scale that will accurately measure the amount of pull that you want on your trigger, and the right hones to use. Your trigger pull should be crisp, with little, if any, over-travel. Unlike a rifle, where over-travel allows you to squeeze the trigger, your shotgun trigger is slapped, with a quick motion.

CAST-OFF

The last of the gun-fitting adjustments is cast-off (or cast-on). You may never have heard of it, but in European countries, especially England, a great deal of importance is attached to it. Cast-off is the lateral deviation of the butt of the stock from the line of sight. It is supposed to enable you to face your target squarely and to minimize the need to incline your head.

I do not like to argue with my European colleagues, but it is an adjustment for which I have found very little, if any, need. And I have fitted an awful lot of shooters. Only a heavy-shouldered, bull-neck shooter really needs any cast-off at all. My personal feeling is that you have enough problems with drop at heel and comb and length of pull, so forget about cast-off unless you're Henry the Eighth.

4

BASIC PRINCIPLES OF SKEET

ALL right, you've got a gun now, and hopefully it fits. Let's talk about how you put it to use.

The firing of a single shot at a single skeet target looks easy when an expert does it, and it is easy, too— *if* you know what you're doing and have established sound shooting habits. Nonetheless, it is also a highly complex action that involves many component elements: you must establish both a stance in relation to the gun, and a position in relation to the spot at which you expect to break the target; you must swing back to a hold position, call for the bird, pick it up with your eyes, start your swing, establish your lead, break the target, and complete your follow-through, and there is a right way and a wrong way to do all of these things. We'll discuss each of these elements in sequence, but first, let me reemphasize that distinction between position and stance.

Position, as I use the term, is the direction in which you are facing in relation to where you expect to break the target, and stance is the attitude of your body once you've taken your position. It is quite possible to have good position and an unorthodox stance and still become a great shooter. For example, Dick Shaughnessy and Ed Calhoun both had unorthodox stances. By always taking the right position, however, they both became great champions. On the other hand, no matter

(Left) Correct position, stance and gun fit. The left leg is advanced, the knee just slightly "cracked" or bent; the right leg is fully extended, but the foot is still flat on the ground. There is a slight forward bend at the waist. The gun is correctly in the shoulder pocket, with the cheek snugly on the stock. The right hand holds the gun; the left hand, positioned towards the rear of the fore-end, is relaxed but firm. (Right) A poor stance common with new shooters: the left knee is bent too much and the shooter is leaning into the shot too much, resulting in poor use of the left arm and right leg. From this position shooters tend to roll with out-going targets, and not being relaxed, often jump their targets.

how perfect your stance may be, if your position is wrong, you have halfway missed the target even before you call for it. The reason is obvious—position governs your swing and follow-through, and thus you must give it a great deal of attention. Stance controls the ease and comfort of your body while you are shooting, but position controls whether or not you hit anything, and thus your score.

(Left) Another common poor stance—the shooter will squat even more when he swings. Body movement will give the sensation of swinging, but too slowly since the right leg has no leverage, and the shooter must use his arms, which is very tiring. Sooner or later he will end up facing the target opening too much. (Right) Good stance, but poor position. This shooter is facing too far past the point where he should break the target, which will prevent him from using his right leg properly and make him very apt to overswing, getting ahead of the target and then having to wait for it. As his feet are in line, he will also tend to roll at the end of his swing, pulling his head off the comb.

Perfect skeet-shooting position, viewed from an unusual angle. Note that the shoulder pocket is at right angle to the butt of the stock, and that the head stays relatively upright even though it is snugly on the comb.

STANCE

Correct stance should be approximately the same for everyone: left foot forward, right foot out to the side and slightly back. The left knee should be slightly bent, the right leg always straight. (This prevents rolling, and gives you something on which to push and start your swing.) Lean slightly forward at the waist, putting most of the weight on the ball of the left foot. The arms should be almost level with the height of the gun, but not uncomfortable. The left hand should be just back of the center of the forearm. Bring the right shoulder up and forward in order to create a pocket for the butt of the shotgun. Now lower your head onto the comb of the stock. That takes care of the main ingredients of stance. The only questions that remain are whether you mount the gun before or after calling for the bird, and whether you shoot with one eye open, or with both. These are details, but important and controversial ones, and we'll come back to them at the end of this chapter. But first, let's look at your position, which is the real key to the whole game.

POSITION

Correct position is much less simple than correct stance, for while the basic principles are the same for everyone, their application varies according to the particular shooter's reflex speed and ability to swing. For example, a shooter who has trouble picking up the outgoing targets, such as a novice or an older person, must take a position that will allow him to break the targets relatively late in their flight, yet allow enough room for an adequate follow-through. If he were to position himself like a AA shooter who breaks his targets before they reach the crossing point, he will find that he has run out of swing before he catches up with the bird. His left arm will bind the swing, stop the gun, and pull his head off the stock. A mistake that many shooters make is thinking that all the targets should be broken over the target crossing point. Actually, there are only two targets that you might *consider* breaking over the crossing point, and these are Station 4 High and Low.

Let me give you a simple rule about where to break your birds: You should break all of the outgoing targets before they reach the stake or crossing point, and never break an incoming target until it has passed the crossing point. After all, it's coming right to you. Why shoot it at 30 yards when you can let it get a lot closer and make sure of the hit? If it were a duck, you'd let it come in until you could shoot it so that it would fall in the boat.

Let me add one proviso to this rule, however: shoot the target as soon as you are on it. Never try to pick

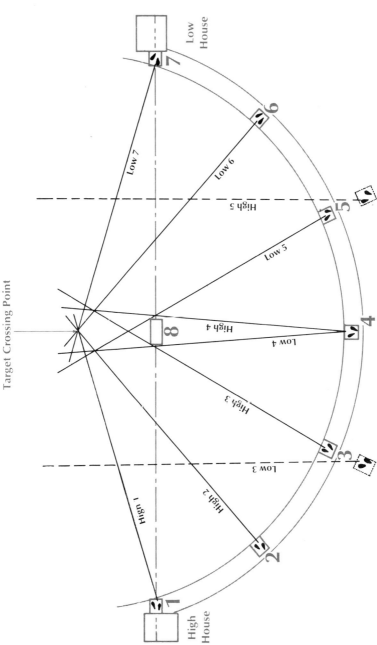

Diagram showing the correct facing position for all shots, Stations 1 through 7. In principle, you always face **just past** the point at which you expect to break the target, thus allowing for follow-through. Note the change of foot position on Stations 3 and 5 for the incomers, insuring a longer lead and extended follow-through.

a spot to shoot your target. If you get on it quickly, shoot it quickly. If you are a little late, shoot it late. Shooting both trap and skeet is largely a matter of position. In each game, there is a moment of truth when you are on the bird and it's time to pull the trigger. The point at which this spot will occur depends on your position. For example, if you wanted to break the target over the low house, you would position yourself so that you would be facing the low house.

For the experienced shooter, then, the correct position of where to break the target is already determined, but it varies according to the direction the bird is traveling. The correct position to face for all your outgoers is just short of the target crossing point. For all of the in-comers, it will be a point after the target crossing point.

The degree on either side of the stake will be modi-fied, as I said earlier, by your timing and reflexes. But above all, shoot the target where you're on it. It is not necessary that you alter your position for the high house or low house on each station so that you walk all over the shooting pad. This won't help your shooting.

There are only two positions at which I'd make a slight change for your second shot, Stations 3 and 5. On Station 3, after shooting the high house target, you should swing just a little more to the left before calling for the low house. This insures enough follow-through to take care of the long lead that this bird requires. After shooting the high house target on Station 5, you should face slightly more to the left for the low house. Here again, you are changing position to allow for the follow-through on the low house. On the other stations, you just reset yourself for the second bird.

When shooting doubles, think of them as if you were shooting singles. Position yourself to kill the first bird. You must face correctly to shoot it. In most tournaments, if you don't kill the first bird, you are out of the game

Correct foot positions for Station 3 (above). Station 3 is one of the two places on the skeet field where the foot position should change between the two singles. Left picture shows the position for the high house target, right the slight turn to the left before calling for the incomer, to insure the long follow-through this target requires and prevent stopping the swing.

Correct foot positions for Station 5 (below), the only other station at which a change is required between the two singles. Left picture shows the correct position for the high house incomer, right the shift to the left that gives the right leg the added leverage it needs to catch the fast-moving outgoer. Note that both positions allow for a long lead and plenty of follow-through.

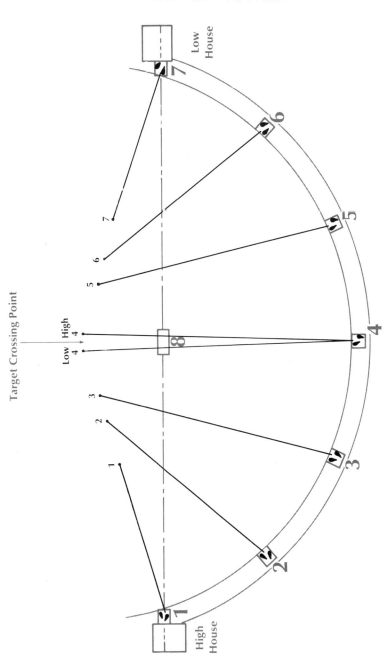

Target Crossing Point

Low House

High House

Low High

Diagram showing the approximate point at which all outgoing targets for Stations 1 through 7 should be broken. Try to break the outgoer before it reaches the target crossing point; the further it goes, the harder it gets.

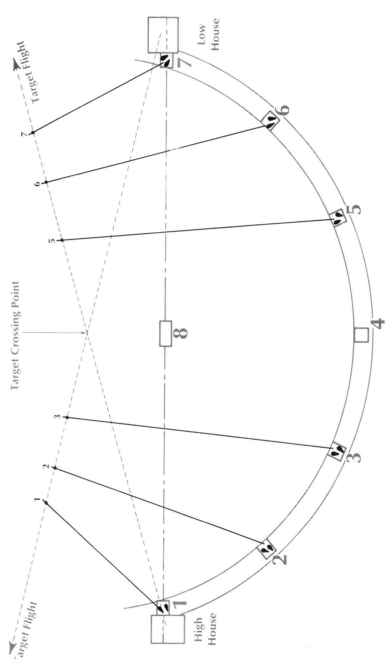

Target Flight

Target Crossing Point

Target Flight

High House

Low House

Diagram showing where to break all incoming targets. In principle, let the incomer come to you, and break it after it has passed the crossing point. Waiting on incomers makes hitting them a bit easier. This is not true for outgoers. Station 4 is omitted, since both targets are considered outgoers.

anyway. Too many people miss doubles by thinking too much about the second bird before they have broken the first bird. The minute you walk on the stand to shoot doubles, tell yourself that you are shooting only a single bird. Position yourself accordingly. Once you've shot the first bird, then swing around and shoot the second bird. If you position yourself to take the second bird, you'll miss the first, and where are you?

I always try to think of it as if I were hunting. If I kill the first bird, I'll have something to eat. If I kill the second bird, my partner will eat. So, I kill my bird first and then worry about his. Actually, the second shot in doubles is much easier than the first simply because you do not have time to think about it. You simply swing, point, and pull.

Position, then, is the most important single factor in skeet shooting. It is like the keel of a ship or the foundation of a building—everything else is built upon it. The correct position is to face just past where you expect to break the targets. If you are a beginner, concentrate on your position and not your final score. If you are an experienced shooter having a slump, check your position at each stand. For position is the real key to shooting success; if every hunter could have positioned himself correctly for each shot in the field, our supply of quail, pheasant, and grouse would have been shot up long ago!

HOLD POSITION AND PICK-UP

Now that we have squared you away on stance and position, the next step is knowing how to use them to best advantage. After placing your feet so that your body is approximately facing just past where you hope to break the target, you turn from the waist, using your knees as well as shoulders, and swing back toward the trap house from which the next bird is about to come. This is your hold position. Then you look for the bird. This is your pick-up.

There are two places to look for the target. If you are a sustained leader you should look at the target opening; if you are a pass shooter, you should look in the vicinity of the gun barrel. Picking up a target quickly isn't difficult, and the right technique can be easily mastered by both types of shooters. But no shooter, no matter how fast his reflexes, should ever try to shoot a target in a blurred state. If you will keep in mind at all times that you can always catch a target and hit it, but must never get ahead of it and wait on it, then you will have little trouble jumping the target and getting out too far ahead of it.

The secret of seeing the target is to simply look for it. Swing back to your hold position, and tell yourself not to move until you're sure to see the target. After all, you cannot shoot what you cannot see. Once you see the target clearly, as a bird and not a blur, make your move and catch it. Swing your gun to the lead needed and fire.

Hold position is important in skeet because it controls your timing, and timing controls where you break the target. The reason you swing back toward the target opening to pick up the target is to get more time to adjust your swing or timing to the speed of the target.

Once you have established your hold position, you will return to it time after time from habit. When you lay off shooting for a while, you sometimes lose this spot. A few inches one way or the other can easily put you in front of the target too soon or too late. Unfortunately, the hold position, like apparent lead, varies with each shooter's reaction time. Therefore, you must work it out for yourself. Later on, when I discuss each station, I will give you the approximate hold position

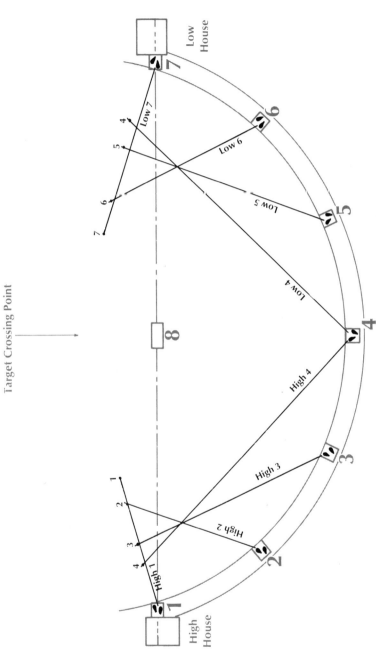

Target Crossing Point

Correct hold or starting position for all outgoing targets, Stations 1 through 7. After taking a dry point just past the spot at which you expect to break the target, you swing back to this hold position before calling for the bird.

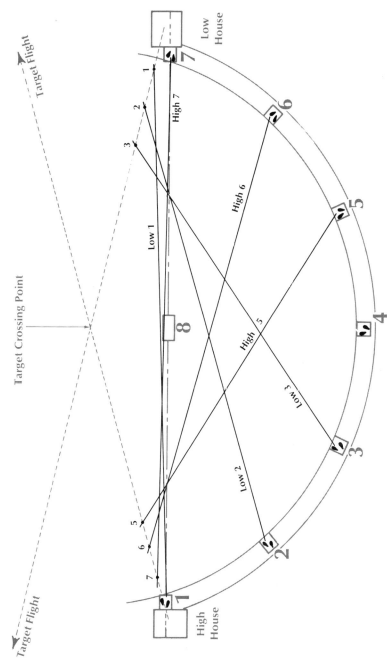

Correct hold position for all incoming targets, Stations 1 through 7. At Station 8 the best hold position is the outside corner of the target opening.

for each shot. These are distances that from years of teaching I have found will work for most shooters. But remember, you must hone them down to a fine edge to suit yourself. Once you have them, never change. Rain, shine, wind, or snow, keep the same hold position.

Hold position controls where you will catch the target, and catch it you must, whether you are a sustained-leader or a pass shooter. But if your hold position is too far in front of the opening, you will get too far ahead of the target, and have to wait for it. Then when you see the proper lead picture and pull the trigger you will shoot behind the target, even though the lead looked correct, because you've had to slow or stop the gun.

On the other hand, if you hold too far back toward the target opening, the target will get so far ahead that you will have to swing twice as fast, trying to catch it. You'll either lose control of your swing, or catch the target so late that you have no swing left. No swing, no follow-through. No follow-through, no busted target.

So remember, the correct hold position for you is one that will allow you to start your swing smoothly, see your lead picture at the right time, and still have some follow-through swing left. You may get by with poor hold positions on incomers and still hit the targets, but not on the outgoers. Thus if you have trouble with High 2 and 3 or Low 5 and 6, check your hold positions. The chances are, that's where the problem lies.

SHOOTING METHODS

There are three ways to shoot a moving object with a shotgun—snap shooting, pass shooting, and sustained-lead. In all three, the shooter shoots exactly the same distance ahead of the target to hit it. The only difference is the method by which he obtains this distance.

We can dispense with snap shooting, which is spot-shooting with a stationary gun. It is primarily used only in field hunting and is not suited for clay target shooting. In pass shooting, the shooter brings his gun up behind the target, catches and passes it, pulls the trigger when he sees the correct apparent lead, and follows through. Sustained-lead is when the shooter picks up the target with his eyes and starts his swing, keeping his gun ahead of the target at all times. When he gets to the correct lead picture, he fires and follows through with his swing.

Both methods are good, if used properly. One is not the least bit better than the other. I have never understood why so many new shooters feel that they must be a sustained-leader to become a champion. Pass shooting seems to be sort of a dirty word. Actually there are a lot more champions who are pass shooters for the simple reason that a larger percentage of all shooters are pass shooters. The reason is that it is easier to learn. I happen to be a pass shooter because I grew up shooting quail and doves. I can shoot a sustained lead, but it's a lot more work, takes constant practice, and I do not break any better scores.

If you are an experienced shooter and use a sustained lead, by all means continue to do so. Get all the practice, especially tournament shooting, you can, so that you will remember exactly what your lead picture is and can shoot accordingly. However, if you are a new shooter, I suggest you stay with pass shooting. It is easier to learn and takes a lot less practice.

A lot of shooters really do not understand the pass-shooting method. They think that you see the target, then swing through it, pulling the trigger as you go by. This is entirely wrong and you will never hit the targets if you try it that way. To pass shoot correctly, you should swing back toward the target opening until your hold position is reached. This should be a spot that, by the time you see the target correctly, it will be slightly ahead of the gun. The gun has already started the swing. When you catch the target, you will stay with it for a fraction of a second. This establishes your timing the same as the target's. You then move on ahead until the desired apparent lead is obtained. Pull the trigger and follow through. This is the easier of the two methods for the simple reason that anyone can point at the target and instinctively pull ahead, but not everyone can figure out what a four-foot lead is going to look like if they have never shot.

LEADS AND HOW TO MAINTAIN THEM

Skeet is actually a simple game, and I have always felt that the more talk there is about leads, the less simple it becomes. For example, if I gave you a rock and told you to hit a car coming down the road, you would throw ahead of it by instinct. If you threw at enough cars, you would soon learn the proper picture to see so that you could hit one. However, as soon as I start telling you what is right for me, telling you exactly at what position you should hit the car, you're apt to stop your swing or get to that spot and wait. On the other hand, there are some shooters who simply have to be told exactly how far ahead they should be in front of the target. These are the shooters who desperately need a coach who can tell them just where they are shooting, in case the fixed lead is not what they think it is.

First, let me make the problem of lead a little simpler. There are two types of lead—horizontal and vertical, or in simpler words, forward and up-and-down. We can do away with the vertical lead by simply telling you to always let the target sit on top of the barrel. If you will do this, I promise that you will never shoot over a

target. Remember, see the whole target at all times. Let
it sit on top of the barrel. It's just as simple as that. Yet
90 percent of all targets missed are shot over, not
behind.

The mathematical lead required on each target is
fixed and calculable. One might think that once the
shooter knew these figures, he could break every target.
However, the actual lead is often quite different from
the apparent lead—apparent to the shooter, that is. The
apparent lead must reckon in the shooter's reaction time
and muscular coordination. One shooter may need a
three-foot apparent lead to break a target. Another
shooter, with faster reflexes, may accomplish it with
an apparent lead of only two feet.

It becomes obvious, then, that tables of computed
actual leads are valuable primarily to show the *relationship* between different target paths and cannot be
depended upon as valid working distances for every
shooter. As an old saying goes, "what's good for the
goose is not necessarily good for the gander."

In another chapter, I will discuss each of the eight
stations. I will give you the approximate lead for each
shot. From long experience, not only in teaching but
also from shooting, I feel that these leads are what most
shooters need to see to break targets, but it will be up
to you to improve on them to suit yourself. I have
actually had students tell me that they have shot six
feet ahead to hit targets at Station 4. Well, if that is
what it takes for you to break them, then do not pull
the trigger until you see six feet. Me, I will stick to a
foot and a half, because that's what I have to see to
break them.

Remember, lead is dependent upon two things, speed
of swing and follow-through. Change either one of these
factors and your apparent lead will change. Your
follow-through will stay fairly constant, but as you

continue to shoot, you become more proficient and find that you can swing faster and get on the target quicker. Then your apparent lead will become smaller.

Where you used to have to see a foot of lead on High 2, you can now see one inch and still break it. You might say that, as you shorten the distance from being a D shooter to an AA shooter, you also shorten the apparent lead.

FOLLOW-THROUGH

Whether you're a pass shooter or sustained-leader, you must follow through after you pull the trigger if you expect to hit the target. The simple explanation for this is that it takes 65 hundredths of a second for you to think, to pull, and for the gun to go off. In that time, the target will move approximately four feet. Stop your swing, and that is exactly how far you will shoot behind the target. In fact, this is the main reason that Mr. Davies created his "around-the-clock" game that we now call skeet. He knew that if he practiced on enough targets, his follow-through would become a natural reaction that would remain with him when he shot in the field. And so it will be with you, if you practice. Practice makes follow-through a habit that comes with instinct. There's no need for swinging your gun on behind you after you have pulled the trigger, as you surely have seen other shooters do. This just gives you one more thing to think about. Be sure to keep moving until you see the target break. This only takes a fraction of a second, but it is probably the most important fraction in the whole round.

Too many shooters, beginners and experienced shots alike, have a tendency to pull the trigger and then jerk their heads up to see if they hit the target. You should be able to see if you have hit the target even with your head on the gun, if you have been leading properly. Your head and eye must stay in line with the end of the barrel until the target falls. Otherwise your tendency to look up will grow with every shot. This action will commence earlier and earlier and can even lead to your lifting your eyes and head before the shot is fired. Proper lead and eye follow-through are just as important as following through with the swing of your gun.

A lot of shooters suffer another form of failing to follow-through, simply because their subconscious mind is capable of working faster than their conscious mind. As they have attained the correct apparent lead, the subconscious mind says, "Stop, that's far enough." So, they stop and pull the trigger before they can think that they must follow through, even though the correct lead is apparent. This is especially true for long leads, such as Low 3, Station 4, and High 5. Although he may have been the right distance ahead of the bird when he was swinging, he is now two or more feet behind the target. There is no way that the bird and the shot will ever meet. In his mind, the shooter honestly believes that he was ahead of the bird. He missed, so he was sure that he overled the target. In reality, he stopped still and was behind the bird when he fired.

This is probably the most common fault—failure to follow through—both in the field and skeet shooting. I have seen country boys who could kill quail as fast as they popped out of the bush, but were lucky to average two doves to a box of shells. The simple explanation for this is that quail move so fast that the shot and follow-through were over before the shooter had time to think. On the dove, however, there is ample time to see the lead picture, judge it to be correct, and stop the swing.

And so it is for skeet shooting. I have seen many beginners who could hit the fast outgoing targets at

Station 2, and Station 5 or 6, and yet miss the easy incomers at 1, 2, and 3, simply because they had too much time to think and see the target and stop the gun.

Some shooters, especially beginners, stop the gun for fear that it will shoot too far ahead of the target. Let me assure you, you *never* shoot too far ahead of a target. Well, hardly ever. If you think you are too far ahead, pull the trigger anyway. Your shot string is about twelve feet long, and the target can always run through the tail end of it. I have never seen a target turn around and go back through a shot pattern. So stay out in front and keep moving.

The best thing to do about follow-through is not to think about it, to concentrate on something else—seeing the target, starting your swing, getting the correct lead, pulling the trigger. Get enough practice and your follow-through will become an instinctive action that you will never have to think about.

Now that we've discussed all the basic principles, let's turn back to those two controversial details, one eye versus two, and the dropped stock versus the shouldered gun. Let's talk about eyes first.

ONE EYE, OR TWO?

I can't count the number of times I've been asked whether a shooter should keep both eyes open, or only one. And if I had a box of shells for every time I've heard the statement made that you've got to shoot with both eyes open to be a top shot, I'd be able to practice all year without buying a shell. So before we go any further, let me get one thing straight—you can become just as good a shooter using one eye as you can using two. You just might have to work a bit harder. (It takes a combination of many things to make a skeet champion, but shooting with both eyes is not one of them.) As an example, Julia Armour, whom I've had the pleasure of teaching, has won many women's championships, including the High-Overall Championship of the World. And she shoots with one eye closed. Henry Joy, one of the early founders of skeet, lost his right eye in an accident. He changed to shooting left-handed with the only eye he had left and became a champion. There are many other examples. So don't blame your poor scores on the fact that you might be a one-eyed shooter.

Let me try to explain this eye business a bit further. Everyone has a master eye. This has nothing to do with the optical strength of either eye. You can have 20/60 vision and still have a master eye in the weaker of the two eyes. With both eyes open, your binocular vision shows you the object. If you point your finger at the same object, your monocular vision takes over and aligns your finger with the object. The only way that you can control your monocular vision is by closing one eye.

Once you mount the gun to your shoulder, monocular vision takes over. It's like pointing the finger, and the master eye points the gun. The other eye goes along just for the ride. The only time that the second, or non-master eye does any work is when you are hunting. With binocular vision (both eyes) you are capable of seeing to the extreme right or left, even though you may be looking straight ahead. Should a bird flush from either side, you see the movement, turn, and make the shot.

To illustrate, try this little test. Raise your arms straight out to the side. Now, while looking straight ahead, move your fingers. You should be able to see them move. Now, close one eye and move the fingers on that side. You can no longer see the movement. With your eye closed, slowly bring your arm forward. Stop as soon as you can see the hand. With one eye closed, then, you would never see a bird in this area if you were hunting. However, when shooting skeet you know exactly where to look for the target. Therefore, you do not need this wide field of vision and it is not a handicap in the least to shoot with one eye closed.

A surprising number of shooters aren't even aware of eye dominance, but one eye is normally dominant over the other when picking up an object and pointing it out. Usually, eye dominance corresponds to body dominance—a right-handed person usually has a dominant right eye, a left-handed person a dominant left eye. Occasionally, dominance will shift back and forth, with no established dominance existing. In extreme cases, there is cross-dominance—the left eye dominating in a right-handed person, interfering with his ability to aim and point a gun mounted to his right shoulder whenever he has both eyes open.

An easy way to determine your eye dominance is to take a clay target and knock out the center. Hold it in your right hand, extend it to arm's length, and close the left eye. With your right eye, center the hole on an object in the distance. Then open your left eye. If the hole jumps to the right of the object, your left eye is the master eye. If, on the other hand, the object stays in the hole, then your right eye is the master eye.

Once you determine which is your master eye, you should do one of three things. First, if you're right-handed and your right eye is the master eye, try to shoot with both eyes open. After all, you have two eyes, so try to use them. However if you find this confusing, try closing the left eye. Sometimes it is easier for a beginner to align the barrel and the target with one eye closed.

Second, if you're right-handed and your left eye is the master eye, you must close it. The correct and best way to do this is to keep both eyes open until you see

A convenient way to check your eye dominance is to knock the center out of a clay target and then, with your left eye closed, frame some object with the target—in this case the palm tree. If the object stays put when you open both eyes, your right eye is dominant; if it jumps to the left, your left eye is. Double-check by aiming at the palm tree with your right eye closed. If you are left-eyed, the tree will stay in place.

the target. Then close the left eye as you swing the gun. If you find this confusing, then just close the left eye when you mount the gun to your shoulder. Do not open it until after the shot has been completed.

Finally, if you are right-handed and your left eye is your master eye, and you cannot close it, you must either learn to shoot left-handed, or put a patch over your left eye. I prefer the former method. If you have never shot right-handed, it only takes a few rounds to learn to shoot left-handed. If you do decide on a patch, however, be sure to remove it between stations. This will prevent your right eye from becoming strained and blurred halfway through the round.

Perhaps the best solution for this type of shooting is one worked out by George Leishear, President of the Florida Skeet Shooting Association. He added a hinged, opaque lens to the left side of his shooting glasses, which can easily be flipped over the left lens just before he takes the shooting station.

THE DROPPED STOCK, PRO AND CON

Now let's turn to the most controversial subject in skeet—should the gun be shouldered before you call for the bird, or only after you've started your swing? In other words, should you call for the bird with a shouldered gun, or with a dropped stock?

In principle, there is only one correct stock position when you're not actually swinging on a bird, and that is with the gun off the shoulder, in about the same kind of ready position you'd use if you were hunting grouse or quail. In practice, however, the correct stock position *for you* is the one with which you can break the most targets.

Sure, skeet shooting was designed originally as a means of improving field shooting. But like a lot of other things, it has outgrown its original function and taken on new meanings. Golf used to be a walking game, but for many players it's a riding game today, even though they call it by the same name.

So it is with skeet. Probably half of our skeet shooters today have little intention of hunting. And so they may fairly ask, "Then why should I call for the bird with the stock dropped from my shoulder?"

The best answer to that is, "Because it might help you break more targets, or break the same number more easily." But then again, it might not. I shoot with a dropped stock myself, and in general, I think more shooters can break more targets more easily that way. Just as a note, if you take the time to check the record, you'll find that about 97 percent of the skeet champions are off-the-shoulder shooters. They may not drop the stock as far as I do, but they all drop it. To name a few—Alex Kerr, Kenny Barnes, Jimmy Bellows, Pete Candy (who still holds the world's long-run record), D. Lee Braun, Barney Hartman—well, you get the point.

Correct low-gun or dropped-stock position. The butt of the stock is just visible below the left elbow, the left hand well back. The head is pushed slightly forward, but relatively erect. The end of the barrel is at eye level, the eyes looking directly over it and the target flight line. The slight bend at the waist will enable the stock to return quickly and accurately to the shoulder pocket.

Let me take a minute here to explain why so many other shooters shoot with the gun mounted to the shoulder today. It is simply that they learn to shoot with it there. This is a correct beginning. Early in their education as a shooter, it gives them one less thing to think about or interfere with their concentration. With it there, there is less chance of bruising the shoulder, and they initially hit more targets.

Even after they have learned, however, they never take the gun off their shoulder because nobody teaches them how to take it off. Consequently, they are afraid that they will regress if they take it off. And it is true, they will. But once they do make the change and take the time to become adjusted to it, the vast majority will be able to shoot 5 or 6 percent better. The reason is simple. They develop a better sense of timing and learn to concentrate on the end of the gun and the bird, overcoming the tendency to aim down the barrel. Finally, they see the bird sooner and get a lot more fun out of their shooting.

As I said earlier, however, the best stock position for *you* is the one with which *you* can shoot your best and break the most targets. Just because Tom, Dick, and Harry shoot a certain way doesn't necessarily mean that it is also the best way for you.

Some shooters simply do not have the reflexes or temperament to shoot with the shotgun shouldered. Others feel the same way about the off-the-shoulder position. Both can be better shots if they keep their own style. Unless you are an AAA shooter, then, there is always room for improvement. And remember that improvement does not always mean a higher score, it can mean many things—you still break the same score but it becomes a lot easier to do it; you get more pleasure out of breaking the same score; or, you smash your targets instead of just chipping them.

Lefthand picture shows correct mounted-gun position. Stock is well in the shoulder pocket, and up on the shoulder. Head is erect, eyes looking right over the end of the barrel for target. Picture on the right shows the correct low-gun, or dropped-stock position, to use after taking dry point before calling for the target. The gun is first pushed out away from you, and then only the butt is lowered, the gun pivoting on the left hand. This leaves the end of the barrel in the same position, with the line of sight right over it, at the flight line. The head must remain in the same position it was in before the stock was dropped. Note the similarity in the stance, position of the head, and where the gun is pointing.

If you are not satisfied with the way you are shooting now try doing something different with the stock. You may be surprised with the results. At the least, you will have eliminated a doubt in your mind as to which way is your way.

If you plan to try the dropped stock position, do the following: First, assume the correct stance and mount the stock correctly in the shoulder pocket. Now shove the gun slightly forward (so that it will not drag on the shoulder), and drop the stock from the shoulder five or six inches. The butt should just be visible below your right elbow. Keep the barrel just below the trap opening, keep your eyes always looking over the end of the barrel for the target. Call for the bird and bring the stock up to your shoulder *as* you swing, not before.

If you are going to try keeping the gun shouldered, be sure you have it correctly in the shoulder pocket, and keep your left hand well back on the forearm. Do not try to look down the rib for the target. Keep the end of the barrel in your line of sight. Do not start your swing until you see the target.

If you're changing styles, I suggest that you practice at first only on the incoming targets, Low 1, 2 and 3 and High 5, 6 and 7. This will give you enough time on the targets to adapt yourself to the new style and at the same time let you hit enough targets to maintain your confidence.

If the change is worth trying, be sure to give it a *good* try, nothing half-hearted. Once you make up your mind to try it, stay with it long enough to give it a fair chance. And for heaven's sake, don't try to change everyone else over to your new way just because it works for you!

To conclude this chapter, let me remind you of one simple fact—in skeet, it's not how you hit the target, but how often. First, perfect the physical factors, like gun fit, stance, and position. Then concentrate on breaking each target as you get to it. It's sort of like the man who had a bird dog for sale. When a fellow asked to see the dog's registration papers, the owner picked up his gun, called the dog, and walked out of the house. In a few minutes he returned with six quail. He threw them on the table and said: "There are his papers."

When someone asks you how you shoot, just point to the 100 straight on the scoreboard and say, "That's how I shoot."

5

STATION-BY-STATION ANALYSIS: SINGLES

AT this point, we've reviewed every physical factor in skeet shooting that can be controlled. We've discussed guns, shells, clothing, and the basic principles of hitting flying targets. The only things left are the psychological factors, such as concentration, and the knowledge of how to use all this information on the skeet field.

The psychology of shooting is so important that I have devoted pages to it later in the book. So for the present, let's pick up our guns and shells and stroll out to the skeet field so that I can analyze each station for you, one by one. I'm going to start off by showing you how to break all the singles, and then deal with doubles in the next chapter, following the traditional form of skeet instead of the "speed-up" system recently adopted as the regulation form. (In speed-up skeet, the doubles at Stations 1, 2, 6 and 7 are shot following the singles, before leaving the station. This is actually easier shooting, but it's probably less confusing to learn how to break each target individually before trying for two.)

Before we start, let's briefly review our general rules:

Above all, remember that the key to successful skeet shooting is position, as explained in the previous chapter. You'll hit targets even by accident if you are facing in the right direction, because correct position sets up your follow-through. The correct position to face is always *just past* the point at which you expect to break your target. Plan to hit all outgoers (High 1, 2 and 3 and Low 5, 6 and 7) *before* they reach the target crossing point, and never break an incomer (Low 1, 2 and 3 and High 5, 6 and 7) until *after* it has passed the stake.

Never spot-shoot—if you try to pick a spot, you'll stop the gun. If you're on the target quickly, shoot it quickly; if you're a little late, shoot it late. You can't shoot them all in the same place. But basically, by remembering to shoot the outgoers early and the incomers late, always on *your* side of the stake, you'll keep your timing consistent.

Remember that skeet targets are basically falling targets, so you must always stay under the target. Your gun muzzle should never be above, or even with, the target. Your pattern might break an occasional bird for you, but most of the time you'd overshoot. *Let the target sit right on top of the barrel.*

Remember that even though all targets start off the same way all the time (aimed 15 feet above the target crossing point, and always at the same speed), you must always be prepared for deviations. Both mechanical and atmospheric variations cause wide deviations in legal targets. So, *be prepared to shoot them all.*

Finally, remember that hold position and lead are personal factors with every shooter, due to variations in individual physique and temperament. Whether you are fast or slow, you can hit them all if you learn your own personal timing and use it consistently. But your own timing is something you'll have to work out by yourself, for yourself. The "recommended" leads and hold positions you'll see below are just rough reference points.

All set? Let's walk over to the high house and call for a couple of targets, just to see how they're flying today. In particular, we want to notice whether or not the birds are traveling right over the stake, and not to one side or the other, and to observe what effect the prevailing wind, if any, is having.

Everything looks pretty normal, so slip one shell into your gun, push off the safety, and bark out a snappy "pull." Well, you got a piece of it, anyway. But now, let me tell you what you *should* have done.

Station 1   High House

The two most maddening misses on a skeet field are your first shot—High 1—and your last, if you'd gone straight till then. They both kill your straight, and there's not much excuse for either one. Of the two, High 1 is often the worse, for thinking about it often sets up more misses, and instead of breaking 24 you end up breaking 19 or 20. It's also one of the commonest misses on the field. Let's take a look at how the shot should be handled, and then review some reasons why it's missed so often.

HOW TO HIT HIGH 1

To shoot High 1 correctly, you must first assume the correct stance, with your right leg fairly straight and most of your weight on your left leg. Slightly bend your left knee. Make sure that your right foot is back and 8 to 10 inches to the side of your left leg. Now, point the shotgun directly over the target crossing point

STATION 1 — HIGH HOUSE

and high enough so that you can intercept the target
about 20 feet from the house. Do not hold high with
the idea of coming down, or hold low with the idea of
coming up on this target. Hold right at the flight line.
Keep your eyes focused beyond the end of the barrel,
right where you think the target will appear. Be alert
and ready. Watch for the target. When it appears in
front of the gun and is sitting on the end of the barrel,
shoot. Keep your head on the stock and follow through.
Above all, do not lift your head and look up as you
pull the trigger. Always break this target before it
reaches the target crossing point.

This is one of the two stands where correct stance is
of utmost importance. Lean slightly forward at the
waist, so your head will rest comfortably on the stock
and stay there. Leaning back at the waist will result
in shooting over this target, as it is constantly falling.

WHY YOU MISS HIGH 1

High 1 is one of the most deceiving and most frequently missed shots on the field, by both top shooters and beginners. Good shooters miss this target because they get careless and are not ready, hold the muzzle too low, or look away when they pull the trigger. Novice shooters, on the other hand ride the target too far out, have a forced stance, hold the gun too high when calling for the target, or are just plain scared to death.

This is one of the stations at which you must be alert and ready the instant you call for the target, for the simple reason that there's no time for recovery. Your first reaction must be correct. The longer you look at this target, the more your eyes are apt to look away from the barrel and at the target alone, which results in shooting over it. Never ride out High 1; shoot it as soon as you're on it.

Another common mistake on High 1 is the tendency to look away once the trigger has been pulled. It is possible to do this on an angled shot such as 3 or 4, but never on a straightaway. Remember, if you keep your head on the gun, you could break the target clear across the field—if you keep pointing at it. So, hold just at the flight line. As soon as you see the target, pull the trigger and follow through.

Station 1   Low House

This is the first of your incoming targets, and you've got no excuse to miss any of them. After all, outgoers get harder as they move away from you, but incomers are coming toward you and getting easier. You've got plenty of time to pick the target up, see what you're going to do, get your lead, pull the trigger, and follow through. Don't make this a hard shot by snapping at it

only a few feet out of the house, or riding it out until it has passed you.

HOW TO HIT LOW 1

To shoot Low 1 correctly, you don't change your stance and position from High 1. Point the gun halfway between the high house and the target crossing point, just at the flight line of the target. Swing back to your hold position, which is just outside the target opening. Give a good sharp call. Be sure you do not move until you see the target. Keeping your eyes focused just over the end of the barrel, pick up the target and start your swing. Bring the target on in halfway between the high house and the target crossing point. Swing approximately a foot ahead, pull the trigger, and follow through.

WHY YOU MISS LOW 1

Here again, if an expert misses Low 1, it's usually because he's gotten careless. Sometimes good shooters will shoot too fast, which results in stopping the gun, or hold so far out in front of the house that they must wait for the target and never get their swing going. Beginners tend to miss this target either by swinging too fast, getting ahead of the target and stopping to wait for it, or by forgetting to keep their head on the gun as they make the long swing from the low house to the point beyond the stake where they try to break the bird.

Station 2   High House

Your basic stance must be a matter of good habit and must remain the same on every station. (If you can't remember the correct stance, go back and reread Chapter 4 again.) Position changes, but not stance. High house 2 is one of the most feared and hated shots on the skeet field, and yet it is not a hard shot. I sometimes think this is simply because the first "fast" target a novice shooter sees is High 2. For the rest of his life he's afraid of it. But once you learn to shoot the bird correctly, it's just as simple as an incomer.

HOW TO HIT HIGH 2

To shoot High 2 correctly, take a position pointing the gun directly over the target crossing point. Swing back until you have reached the correct hold position, at right angles to the flight of the target. Keep the muzzle just under the imaginary flight line of the target, and keep your eyes focused over the end of the barrel to a point just in front of the trap house. Do not look at the opening. Be alert and ready, for this is the second of your no-return birds; your first decision must be right. Above all, do not move the gun until you see the target. Remember, you cannot shoot what you can-

STATION 2—
HIGH HOUSE

Correct dry point for Station 2 high house. The gun is pointed exactly over the target crossing point, and is elevated only to shoulder height. Note that the left hand is well back on the fore-end, so that the swing can be started with a quick push. From here, the shooter swings back to a hold position at right angles to the target flight line, drops his gun butt and calls for the target.

not see. Begin moving the gun with a quick push of the left arm and a downward push from the right leg. Catch the target, and as soon as you see daylight between the barrel and the bird, pull the trigger and follow through. Although the lead picture here is one foot, your swing is so fast that if you pull the trigger when you see daylight, by the time the gun goes off you will have the one foot necessary to break the target. A great many shooters overlead this target, not realizing that if they see a foot of daylight with a fast swing, by the time they pull the trigger they will be at least two feet ahead of the target.

This is a typical outgoing target, and should be shot before it reaches the target crossing point. Remember, though, that this is primarily just a positive thought to keep you from lally-gagging around and riding the target too far. You should actually shoot any target when you're on it. If you're not on it by the time it reaches the target crossing point, don't shoot it; shoot it only when you see the correct picture. However, *trying* to shoot it before it gets to the target crossing point will insure that you have some follow-though left, in case you need to make a correction. Here again, let the bird sit on top of the barrel at all times. There's a tendency on the part of some AA shooters to shoot the target too fast. There's no advantage in shooting any target before your pattern has opened up to its potential.

WHY YOU MISS HIGH 2

High 2 is more of a chop shot than it is of a swing shot. The trick to making it easy is to use the left arm and the right leg. By pushing over with the left arm and down with the right leg, you get the added momentum needed to catch this fast-moving target and make it as simple as any other shot.

Most experienced shooters miss it for one of three

reasons. They unknowingly begin to swing around and face the target opening too much, hold the muzzle of the gun too far out in front of the target opening, or get so keyed up that they jump the bird. Beginners are more often unable to swing fast enough and shoot too late; or they face too far to the right, or look up as they pull the trigger.

Station 2   Low House

Low 2 is almost a repeat of Low 1. The only difference is that it requires another foot of lead, and your hold position should move slightly farther out in front of the target opening.

STATION 2 — LOW HOUSE

HOW TO HIT LOW 2

To shoot low house 2 correctly, there is no need to change your position; just reset yourself. This a left-quartering incomer that should be broken after it passes the stake, about halfway between the high house and the target crossing point. Your stance remains the same. Point the gun halfway between the target crossing point and the high house. Now swing slowly back to the low-house opening. Stop the muzzle about six feet outside the opening; this is your hold position. Keep your eyes focused on the end of the gun and the chute. Call for the target, but again, do not move until you see it. Swing with the target. Catch it, follow it, and move ahead, timing your swing so that you catch the bird after it passes the target crossing point. Pull two feet ahead. Pull the trigger and follow through.

Although you should never shoot an incomer too quickly, neither should you ride it too far. As soon as you see your lead picture, pull the trigger and follow through, breaking the bird about halfway between the high house and the target crossing point.

WHY YOU MISS LOW 2

As I said, you should never miss an incomer, and that is just why AA shooters miss incomer 2. They forget about it, and take the target for granted. There's not a target on the field that you can take for granted. You must shoot each and every one.

Good shooters make the following mistakes: They try to shoot the target before it has passed the target crossing point, hold too far in front of the house and wait on the target, or start to walk away before the shot it finished. Beginners usually miss because of poor position, facing too much toward the house, or maintain no lead, that is, they shoot right at the target and forget that here the lead is from 1½ to 2 feet.

Station 3   High House

High house 3 is exactly like High 2, except that you have more time to make the shot. You must remember, though, that you cannot make this shot as quickly as you do High 2, for the simple reason that you must see a foot of lead before you pull the trigger.

HOW TO HIT HIGH 3

To shoot Station 3 high house correctly, take a position in which your gun is pointed exactly between the

STATION 3 — HIGH HOUSE

target crossing point and Station 8. Take the correct stance, with most of your weight on your left leg, and slightly bend the left knee. When you swing back to your hold position, pivot on the left knee. The right leg is always straight; this prevents rolling with the shot. Your hold position on this shot should be slightly closer to the target opening then it was on Station 2— approximately fifteen feet from the opening is about right. Keep your eyes focused over the end of the gun at the spot where you expect to first see the target. The gun muzzle should be just below the chute.

I cannot repeat too often, do not move until you see the target. Once you see it, start your swing, catch the bird, and pass it. When you see a foot of daylight, pull the trigger and follow through. Although you have more time on this shot, you should start your swing slightly faster, to insure that you catch the target and see the foot of daylight needed to break it before it reaches the target crossing point. Once you are in position, keep telling yourself that this is just like Station 2 except I swing back a little farther, swing a little faster, and see a little more daylight. It's as simple as that.

WHY YOU MISS HIGH 3

The first big mistake made by AA shooters on this station is snapping at the bird before they've got their lead. The second is holding too far in front of the house and waiting on the target. The third is poor position. Good shooters have a tendency to key around and face the house too much, thinking they will get the target sooner. However, this only binds their swing, stopping the gun and forcing them to shoot behind the bird. Most beginners fail to give enough lead, have poor position and stance, or shoot the target too late. Some tend to stop the swing once they see the lead.

Station 3   Low House

Although this incoming target is a repetition of Stations 1 and 2, it's one of the trickiest targets on the field. The reason is that your apparent lead picture here does not increase proportionately. Instead of the expected two-foot picture, it jumps to three feet or more. AA shooters will chip and crack this target more than any other one on the field.

HOW TO HIT LOW 3

To shoot Low house 3 correctly, you must change your position. This is one of the two stations where I like to change positions, after shooting the first target,

STATION 3 — LOW HOUSE
Note that the foot position has shifted slightly, so that the shooter now faces well to the left of the target crossing stake.

to shoot the second one. Both feet should be shifted a little more to the left in order to insure a positive follow-through to take care of the large lead that is needed on this station. Your position should face halfway between Station 1 and the target crossing point. Your weight stays on the ball of your left foot and, as you swing back to the low house, you pivot on the left knee. Be sure to keep your shoulders straight. Do not drop the right shoulder. The right leg remains straight, to keep you from squatting or rolling with the shot. Your hold position on this shot should be slightly farther away from the house than it was on Station 2, about twelve to ten feet in front of the opening. Your swing should be slightly down until the muzzle is just below the flight line of the target. Keep your line of sight over the end of the gun and look for the target at all times. Once you see the target, start your swing and get on it. Follow it well past the target crossing point and lead it approximately three and a half feet. Pull the trigger and continue to follow through.

On this station you must swing slightly faster than you did on Station 2 and Station 1 in order to catch the target at the same spot. The target should always be broken halfway between the target crossing point and the high house. Be careful not to face into the house too much on this shot, for it requires a long lead and a lot of follow-through. And regardless of how far ahead you are, never stop the gun. It has been my experience that you can hit this target even if you are four feet ahead.

WHY YOU MISS LOW 3

Here again, AA shooters miss mainly because they shoot too quickly, hold too far in front of the chute, and stop the gun when they catch the target, or, like everybody else, just fail to lead the target enough. Beginners almost always take poor position, facing the house too much, or fail to lead enough because they just cannot believe that you can shoot so far ahead of a target and still hit it.

Station 4   High House

On this station, both targets are considered outgoers and should be shot fairly close to the target crossing stake, never more than three or four feet to either side of it. This station demands the longest lead in the game, but it's not missed as much as Station 3 or Station 5.

HOW TO HIT HIGH 4

To shoot High 4 correctly, take a position facing about three feet to the right of the target crossing point. Some shooters make the mistake of facing right at the target crossing point, which means that you must break the target too soon or you will run out of follow-through and stop the gun. Both targets at this station should be broken almost over the target crossing point, never more than three or four feet to the right or left. When you have your position, point three feet to the right of the target crossing point and swing back to your hold position. This should be slightly closer to the house than at Station 3, about eight or nine feet from the opening. Keep the muzzle just below the flight line of the target or the chute opening. Your line of sight should be over the end of the gun, focused on infinity, at the point at which you expect to first see the target. Do not look at the trap opening; you will see it in your peripheral vision, but you should concentrate on looking in the vicinity of the gun barrel, as this is where you will first

STATION 4 —
HIGH HOUSE

see the target. When you do see the target start your
swing, remembering that you must swing faster here
than you did at 2 and 3 because you must catch the
target at the same point even though you have half the
distance in which to do it. Once you catch the target,
pull ahead two feet, pull the trigger, and continue to
follow through.

Although the lead on High house 4 is three and a
half to four feet, the swing is so fast that an apparent
lead of one and a half or two feet is ample to get
the correct break on this target. Here, again, tell yourself to go back a little farther than at Station 3, start a
little faster, and get a little farther ahead. In this way,
you have three shots that are all tied together instead
of three individual shots. Never doubt your lead picture here. It is almost impossible to shoot too far ahead
of this target. This is one shot where the right leg
should be kept straight at all times. If you bend it,

you will roll over the target, giving you a sensation of moving the barrel when actually all that you are moving is your body, and you will find that you will underlead the target.

WHY YOU MISS HIGH 4

As on Station 3 High, good shooters miss here because they have a tendency to hold too far out in front of the trap opening, take a poor position facing too much toward the house, or start the swing before they have seen the target. Beginners usually miss because they ride the target too far, fail to lead enough, or have very poor position.

Station 4   Low House

Although Low 4 is a much easier shot for right-handed shooters than the high house at Station 4, because of its more natural swing, Low 4 is missed far more frequently by top shooters. The reason for this is that they fail to realize that the low-house target has now become an outgoing target which requires a faster swing. Remember the rule I gave you earlier—break all outgoers before they reach the target crossing stake.

HOW TO HIT LOW 4

To shoot this target correctly, take a position facing three feet to the left of the target crossing point. It is not necessary to face too much to the left on this shot, for the simple reason that your natural swing is to the left and you will have no trouble following through. When you swing back to your hold position, do so by pivoting on the left knee, keeping the weight on the left

STATION 4 —
LOW HOUSE

foot and keeping the right leg straight. Do not drop your right shoulder. If you drop the right shoulder when you make your swing, you will drop it even further, resulting in your pushing the gun over the top of the target. Your hold position on this station should be slightly less than it was on Station 3, or approximately twelve or thirteen feet outside of the target chute.

Again the muzzle of the gun is dropped slightly below the flight line of the target, your line of sight remaining over the barrel, watching for the target. You must never start your swing until you are sure you have seen the target. It's very easy to catch this bird, but it's deadly to get too far ahead and have to wait on it.

As soon as you see the target, start your swing quickly, catch it, pass it, see approximately a one and a half foot lead, pull the trigger, and follow through. Be sure to keep your head on the comb well after the shot has been fired, as the target is rising and so is the gun. If you are not careful your head will come off the stock, resulting in shooting over the target. Although the lead here is three and a half to four feet, the swing has been increased so much that an apparent lead of one foot or a foot and a half will be ample to catch this target and hit it.

A word of warning. I did not say, "Shoot quickly;" I said, "*swing* quickly." If you swing quicker you will catch the target sooner, thereby shooting sooner. But if you think "shoot quicker," you will just pull the trigger sooner, stopping the gun and shooting behind the target. This is a simple target, one that should cause little trouble if you increase the speed of your swing as soon as you reach the Station 4 stand.

WHY YOU MISS LOW 4

The AA shooters miss this target because they fail to speed up their swing, face into the house too much, or look up when the trigger is pulled, probably because the target is rising. Beginners fail to lead the target enough, ride the target too long, and quite often hold in too close to the target chute.

Station 5   High House

The first thing to remember when you get to Station 5 is that the high house has now become an incoming target and should be shot after it crosses the target crossing point. Therefore, your correct position would be to face about twenty feet to the right of the target crossing stake. This will allow for a lot of follow-through to take care of the long lead necessary on this shot. You should also remember that by the time you shoot this target, it will be dropping. Therefore, you

STATION 5 — HIGH HOUSE

must stay under it at all times, letting it sit on top of the gun barrel.

HOW TO HIT HIGH 5

Take a position about halfway between the target crossing point and low house. With the proper stance and with the muzzle of the gun just below the flight line of the target, swing back to the proper hold position. This should be just slightly closer to the house than at Station 4, or just about roughly ten feet to the right of the chute. Keeping your line of sight over the end of the gun barrel, watch for the target. Once you see it, start your swing quickly and catch the target before it reaches the target crossing point. By starting to swing fast, you catch the target quickly and have complete control over it; you can shoot it at any time you wish, and naturally choose to do so after it crosses the target crossing point. Once you catch the target, continue your swing, letting the target sit on top of the gun, pull three feet ahead, pull the trigger, and follow through. Do not ride this target too far. If you do so, the left arm will bind the swing and pull your head off the gun, resulting in your shooting over the target. This is the longest apparent lead on the field, so be sure you see a good three feet of daylight between your muzzle and the bird before you pull the trigger. Better too far ahead than too far behind.

WHY YOU MISS HIGH 5

This target is missed consistently by good shooters simply because they take a poor position. They face the high house too much, thereby binding their swing and stopping the gun. Keep in mind that anything going from left to right is more difficult for a right-handed shooter. Therefore, you must allow for more follow-through. Many shooters also fail to lead the target enough, or get too far ahead and stop the gun because they think the lead is correct. And last, but not least, they hold too far out in front of the chute, anticipating the target.

This target completely baffles the new shooter. He just cannot understand the extreme lead that this target takes, and if he does get that far ahead, he insists on stopping the gun and pulling the trigger. Most of the time he also has a very bad position, which will not allow for the proper follow-through.

High 5 is just as simple and easy as the Station 3 incomer if you do it correctly, and since you have all the time in the world to shoot the target, there's no reason why you cannot do it correctly.

Station 5   Low House

Low house 5 has always been the most frequently missed target on the field. This is hard to understand, as it is a right-to-left shot that gives the shooter the advantage of his natural swing. However, one thing working against the shooter here is that he is shooting a slow, incoming target first and the fast outgoing target afterwards. It is very difficult for the mind to go from slow to fast. On the other side of the field, you shoot the fast target first, and there is less problem in going from fast to slow. On Station 5, you shoot a slow incoming high house target, and fail to speed up sufficiently on the outgoer, resulting in your shooting behind the target.

STATION 5 — LOW HOUSE
Note change in foot position to the left. With the right knee straight, the pivot will be on the left knee. Lean into this shot and keep the left shoulder slightly lower than the right.

HOW TO HIT LOW 5

To take the correct position here, point the gun between the 8 stand and the target marker and let your
feet adjust accordingly. Point the barrel of the shotgun
shoulder high, and check to be sure that you have the
correct sighting plane. Do not point the gun where you
think the target will go; there is an optical illusion here,
and by the time you shoot this target, it will be going
down. Swing back to your proper hold position, which
again will be slightly farther from the house than it
was at Station 4, or just about roughly fifteen feet
in front of the low house chute. Keep the muzzle of
the gun just below the flight line of the target so that
you can see the target the second that it emerges from
the house. Your line of sight should be over the end of
the gun, watching for the target. Your swing back to
the house should be made by pivoting on the left knee,
keeping the weight well on the left foot and left knee.
The right leg should be straight at all times. The left
shoulder drops slightly and the right shoulder stays in
the normal position. Here, again, is a target on which
you must not move until you see the target as a target,
and not as a blur. Swing fast, catch it, pull ahead approximately one foot, pull the trigger, and follow
through. Be sure not to lift your head as you pull the
trigger. This is a rising target, and it's very easy for
the head to come off the comb. Keep in mind at all
times that this is an outgoing target that must be broken
before it reaches the target crossing point.

WHY YOU MISS LOW 5

Most good shooters miss here for the same reason
they miss at Station 4. They take poor positions, facing
too much toward the target chute. They fail to speed

up their swing and fail to follow through on a high-rising target. Inexperienced shooters usually miss because of poor stance, poor position, or riding the target too far. I know from sad experience that he who hesitates at Station 5 low is lost. It cost me the World's 12-Gauge Championship in a shoot-off with Sergeant Glenn Van Buren in Las Vegas, Nevada, in 1948. They say that experience is a hard teacher, and I can still see that bird, flying off intact.

Station 6   High House

When you reach Station 6, you feel you should be able to relax a bit and say, "I'm in like Flynn." But that is the trouble; too many good shooters do just that and end up dropping a target or two on this station. The incomer is an easy quartering right angle. The outgoer is almost a straightaway. It's a simple stand if shot correctly. However, too many people are apt to take it for granted, including yours truly.

HOW TO HIT HIGH 6

To shoot high house 6 correctly, treat it like a right-quartering incomer. Take a position similar to that at Station 5 high house, but face a bit more to right, about halfway between the crossing point and the low house. Keep your right leg straight. Be sure to check your foot position and see that the right foot is not behind the left. If the right foot is too far behind the left foot, you will find yourself off balance when you follow this long incoming target in, and your tendency will be to roll with the shot and shoot over the target. Lean slightly forward at the waist, keeping the weight on the left knee and the ball of the left foot. Keeping the barrel

STATION 6 —
HIGH HOUSE

Note that the high-house position at left faces well to the right of the target crossing stake to allow for a long follow through.

shoulder level, swing back to your hold position, which should be closer to the house than at Station 5.

On this shot I like to hold four feet from the edge of the house. The muzzle of the gun should be pointed just below the opening of the chute. Again, keep your line of vision over the end of the barrel and the opening of the house. Just as on Station 5 High, when you see the target, start your swing quickly, catching the bird before it gets to the target crossing point. Keeping the target just above the barrel, follow it in. When you see a two-foot lead, pull the trigger and follow through. Be sure to keep your cheek on the comb. This is an easy shot to look up on, and the fact that the left arm is holding back on the swing tends to pull the head up.

You should break this target about halfway between the target crossing point and the low house. On this shot, you will run out of left-arm swing almost at the target crossing point so you must pivot on your left knee to keep your follow through going.

High 6 is really an easy shot, but it is a fooler. Over-confidence here can knock you out of the tournament or kill your long run before you realize what's happening.

WHY YOU MISS HIGH 6

Good shooters usually miss this target due to over-confidence or pulling the head off the target, stopping and pulling the trigger, shooting too quickly, which results in stopping the gun, or failing to stay *under* the target correctly. Beginners rarely have much trouble with this target because they have a lot of time to follow it and get the correct lead. If they do miss, it's usually from riding the target too long, poor position and stance, or not keeping the head on the comb when they pull the trigger.

Station 6   Low House

Low 6 is a slight left-quartering outgoer that I'm sure Mr. Davies loved, as it is more like field shooting than any other shot on the field. It is a simple shot, and one that should never give you any trouble if done correctly. Here, as on Station 2 High, you should use your left arm and your right leg to give you the quick start and momentum you need to catch a fast, outgoing target. Although the lead here is about one foot, it is possible as at Station 2 to shoot right at the front edge of the target and still break it.

HOW TO HIT LOW 6

To shoot Low 6 correctly, face right at the target marker. You may be a little uncomfortable when you swing back to your hold position, but when you shoot, you'll not only find that you're comfortable, but you'll also have enough follow-through to break the target. Facing too far to the left of the target marker will cause you either to overlead with an exaggerated swing or to ride the target out too far and shoot it after it crosses the crossing point. Remember, this is an outgoer that should be shot before it reaches the target crossing point. Facing too much to the right of the target crossing point will mean that the target will have to be shot too quickly. Any time you shoot too quickly, you risk the danger of stopping your swing.

Once you have your correct position, swing back to your hold position, which on this stand should be slightly less than a right angle to the flight of the target. Make doubly sure that the muzzle of the gun is just below the imaginary flight line of the target. If you hold higher, it will be possible for the target to come out under the barrel. You will see it too late, and it will throw your timing off or give you a jerky swing. Keep your eyes focused in the vicinity of the gun barrel. Do not look back over your shoulder at the house. As soon as you see the target emerge, start your swing by pulling with the left arm and pushing down on the right leg. Here again, this is a chop shot, not a swing shot. You have to catch this bird quickly to make it an easy shot. So swing quickly. The only way you can do this is by using the left arm and the right leg.

A word of caution here. If you use this method, it will give you so much leverage that when you first try it, you are apt to find yourself too far in front of the bird, and have to wait on it. So remember, when you

STATION 6 — LOW HOUSE

Hold position for the low
house (below) is just
slightly less than a right
angle to the flight line.

see daylight, pull the trigger. Once your swing is
started, catch the target, pull ahead until you see daylight or about six inches of apparent lead. Then pull
the trigger, keeping the head well on the comb of the
gun, and follow through. If possible, never let this
target get past the target crossing point.

WHY YOU MISS LOW 6

Good shooters miss this target quite often because
they shoot ahead of it, unconsciously key around and
face the house too much, which binds the swing, or get
careless and shoot over the target. And last, but not
least, too many of them try to shoot this target too
quickly. Here again, beginners have very little trouble
because this is like a field shot and almost a straightaway. Even if they follow the target out too far, they
usually hit it. Their main problem is usually position
and stance.

Like High 6, this is a target on which you can easily get careless. But with good position and concentration and enough nerve to pull the trigger at the right time, Station 6 can become as easy as Station 7. On Station 5 and Station 6 low house, you must lean into the shot. Make sure that you do not straighten up as you swing. If you do so, you will shoot over the target 90 percent of the time. This is due to an optical illusion. The shooter thinks the target is continuing to rise when actually by the time he shoots it has almost started its downward trend. It is a natural reaction for your body to want to return to an upright position, as that is the way you walk around every day. You must overcome this, however, and lean into this shot if you expect to hit it consistently.

Station 7   High House

Little time need be spent in discussing this station as it is the easiest on the field and causes very little trouble. When it's missed, it's usually just stupidity or carelessness. Like Stations 1 and 8, it is a give-away target. However, once you become a AA shooter it's the give-away easy shots that cause you all the trouble simply because you relax and fail to concentrate. So pay attention on this shot.

HOW TO HIT HIGH 7

Swing back to your hold position just to the right of the target opening. Do not move until you see the target. Swing with the target, letting it sit on top of the gun. Bring it in halfway from the target crossing point to the low house. When you see daylight between the left-hand side of the barrel and the target, pull the trigger

STATION 7 — HIGH HOUSE   **STATION 7 — LOW HOUSE**
The hold position for High 7 (left) is the right-hand corner of the target opening. (Do not hold off the house unless a trap boy is inside.) The hold position for the low house is directly over the target crossing stake, the barrel neither high nor low, but right on the flight line of the target.

and follow through. The lead here is about one foot. However, if you continue your swing and follow through, you can almost shoot at the front edge of the bird.

Remember to keep your cheek on the comb and do not look up. On any left-to-right shot the left arm tends to bind the swing and force the head off the stock. You must remember to pivot on the left leg to keep your follow-through smooth. Do not follow the target too far; it is falling, and riding it can lead to jerking the trigger which can end up in a flinch.

WHY YOU MISS HIGH 7

This target is missed either because it is shot too fast or because the shooter follows it in too long, lifts his head, or is just careless. Your correct position is to face just to the right of the target crossing point. Keeping the gun shoulder level, swing back to your hold position, which on this shot is just to the right-hand side of the target opening. The muzzle should be just below the opening, and your eyes should be focused over the end of the barrel, watching for the target. Never move until you see the target emerge from the house. Remember, you can always catch the target, but you cannot restart your swing if you get ahead and stop.

Station 7   Low House

Although this is another easy target like High 1, it is a straightaway, and any straightaway can be deceiving. (If you have ever shot trap, you will know this to be a fact, as 90 percent of all targets missed at trap are straightaways.) The simple explanation for this is that you can see an angled target quicker. You also have twelve feet of shot string going out in front of the target. On a left angle, you're pushing the gun into your head; on a right angle, you're pushing your head into the gun. On a straightaway, however, there's nothing to keep you from lifting your head off the stock or shifting your eyes away from the muzzle as you concentrate on the bird. Moreover, you only have the diameter of your pattern to help you—about a foot and a half, at this station—instead of that long shot string.

HOW TO HIT LOW 7

To shoot Station 7 correctly, take a position exactly facing the target crossing point. Adjust the gun right over the stake as near the flight path of the bird as possible. It's a good idea to watch the shooter ahead of you to get some idea as to what the flight path is. Keep the right leg straight. Bend the left knee and lean slightly forward into the gun. Your line of sight should be right over the end of the muzzle out into infinity where you expect to see the target.

When you see the target, and by this I mean not a blur, but a target, let it sit on top of the gun. Pull the trigger and follow through until you see the target smash. Do not shoot this target too fast. Give your pattern a chance to open up. See what the target is going to do. It may look spectacular to break a few birds ten or twelve feet from the house, but I can guarantee you there are more targets missed at ten or twelve feet than there are broken. Be sure you are ready when you call, as this is a non-recovery bird. Here again, your first reaction is the only one you get, and it must be correct. So stay awake and shoot the target before it reaches the crossing point.

WHY YOU MISS LOW 7

AA shooters miss the Station 7 outgoer mostly through carlessness, but mostly they don't often miss it. Occasionally they miss it by holding the muzzle of the gun too far below the flight line of the target, or by shooting too fast and looking away as they pull the trigger. Beginners usually don't have much trouble with

Low 7, either. If they muff it, it's usually because they ride it out too far, or fail to keep their eyes both on the end of the gun and the target.

Station 8   High House

When you first start shooting skeet, the two Station 8 shots seem almost like trick shots, by far the most difficult targets on the field. They aren't. In fact, they can be two of the easiest targets on the field, once you know how to shoot them properly. High 8 is the third station, along with High 2 and Low 6, in which the left hand ceases to be a hitchhiker and earns its keep. By starting the swing with the left hand, it's a very simple matter to catch the target and break it halfway between the house and the target crossing point.

HOW TO HIT HIGH 8

To shoot High 8 properly, remember that this bird is a slightly quartering incomer. Take a position facing just to the right of the high trap house. Be sure your stance is the same as on every other station—right foot well to the side, left foot forward. The weight is still on the left leg, the knee slightly bent. The right leg must be kept straight at all times. Do not bend the right leg, for this will result in squatting and pull you off the target.

Your correct hold position is just at the right bottom edge of the opening. The muzzle of the gun should be just below the opening, allowing you to see the bird as soon as it emerges. When you call for the bird, you must be ready. Make sure not to move the gun before you see the target. Start your swing by pushing with the left arm. Keep your eye on the end of the barrel and

STATION 8 — HIGH HOUSE

I hold just below the right corner of the target opening, as shown at left. This target should be broken as soon as the barrel covers it, which should put the break about where shown below.

the bird at all times. Black the target out with your muzzle and pull the trigger. This target should be broken approximately halfway between the high house and the crossing point. If you break the target here, you will utilize the entire length of your shot string and avoid the risk of lifting your head as the gun goes higher.

The principal question about High 8 is whether you should point the gun directly at the opening, or more or less to the right of it. I've seen good shots do both. However, in years of teaching I've found that pointing at the opening enables you to see the target almost as it emerges. Once you see it, you start your swing and catch it, and your timing remains correct. If you hold very far off the opening, even a couple of feet from the house, you must wait on the target and start your swing later. Then you may not have time to catch the target. In any event, holding away from the opening definitely seems more difficult for most pupils. The only time you should hold off the house is when there is a trap boy inside, and you *must* do it then. But not many clubs lack automatic traps these days.

WHY YOU MISS HIGH 8

AA shooters don't miss High 8 often, but when they do, it's usually from shooting too fast. Beginners usually miss because the mind and all composure have left the body, and they either fire without watching the end of the gun and the target, or they follow the target too long.

Station 8   Low House

This is the last of the single shots. It is almost a repetition of the high house target except that here the shot is even easier, for the simple reason that it's a right-to-

STATION 8 — LOW HOUSE

Facing the house. I take a gun point just below the flight line on the left-hand corner of the target opening. Weight is forward, and the right leg straight to prevent rocking back. Swing is mostly with the arms, and the bird is broken as soon as the barrel covers it, well before it reaches the stake.

left shot and the shooter can take advantage of his natural swing to the left.

HOW TO HIT LOW 8

Take your correct position, facing just to the left of the low house, with the correct stance. Keep your right leg straight and your left knee slightly bent. Your weight should be well forward on the left leg. Point the muzzle of the gun directly at the target opening. Keep your eyes focused on the muzzle and the opening. The barrel should be held just low enough in relation to the chute for you to see the target as soon as it emerges. Be sure when you call that you are ready. Do not move until you see the target. Once you see it, start your swing by pulling with the left arm while keeping your eyes on the end of the barrel and the target. Black the bird out and pull the trigger. The target should be broken halfway between the low house and the target crossing point. Do not swing by rocking back or leaning back; this is an arm shot. By moving the left arm, you move the muzzle of the gun twice as fast as you do when you rock back.

WHY YOU MISS LOW 8

Generally you miss Low 8 for the same reasons that you miss High 8. Beginners take too high a gun point on the low house and have to wait for the target, letting it get too high. But the main reason for missing is still loss of composure and jabbing at the target instead of swinging on it.

6

STATION-BY-STATION ANALYSIS: DOUBLES

NOW that we've discussed each of the sixteen singles targets, we've seen every different bird the field can show us. All that remains (except perhaps the optional) is the four pair of simultaneous high- and low-house targets called "doubles."

Contrary to appearances and what you may think, doubles aren't hard. In fact, I've always felt that doubles are easier than singles for the simple reason that on singles you're apt to be a little too careful. On doubles you shoot the shotgun as it was meant to be shot, by swinging, pointing, and pulling the trigger. I know this is true because in teaching beginners I have found that they not only hit doubles better than singles, but they hit the second bird better than the first bird, simply because they're just pointing and pulling.

It's not unusual to see a beginner miss an incomer 1 target, which is the easiest target on the field, and then walk over to Station 2 and break a pair of doubles, which are probably the most difficult doubles in the game. Like a country boy shooting quail, he just points and pulls when he thinks everything is right.

Doubles are shot from Stations 1, 2, 6, and 7. Originally, you had to shoot all singles first (except the optional) and then returned to Station 1 to start your doubles. This is the traditional way, and it's the way I prefer. In this modern day and age, however, most skeet is shot using the so-called speed-up system, in which the doubles at each station where they're shot are pulled immediately after the singles. Speed-up skeet means a saving on traps and personnel (because more people can use less equipment), and there is no doubt that it will end up being the dominant form of the game, in tournaments as well as ordinary weekend shoots.

Some of the changes in skeet rules, such as eliminating the dropped stock and the three-second delay, have helped the game but not the shooter. This is not true with speed-up skeet. I believe that shooting doubles speed-up makes them easier than ever before. The reason is that, having just shot your singles, you ought to be able to remember just what the birds looked like when you shoot your double. Furthermore, if you've broken both singles, it ought to help your confidence. The only danger is a feeling of being hurried. Don't get the idea that just because you're shooting speed-up you must change your timing. Take your time as you reload, concentrate, and then call for your double. After all, speed-up was designed to save non-shooting time, not shooting time.

Whether you're shooting doubles in the traditional sequence or speed-up, there's only one way to handle them correctly: concentrate on the first bird, which *must* be the outgoer, and break it exactly as if it were a single target. Only when you have hit it, and seen it break, should you look for the second target. Swing back and shoot right at it, being careful not to lift your head off the stock or take your eyes off the end of the barrel and the target. Too many good shooters think too much about the second target first. This is apt to change their timing and make them do something different. If you do not kill the first bird, you are out of most tournaments anyway. So kill the first one. Then worry about the second one.

HOW TO HIT STATION 1 DOUBLES

To shoot Station 1 doubles correctly, you should treat the first target as a single bird. Assume the same position and stance as when you shot High 1 singles. Concentrate on the bird just as a single. Hold just below the flight line of the target, keeping your line of vision over the end of the gun, at infinity, where you first

In shooting doubles, the foot position at each station is the same as the foot position for the outgoer single. If you break the outgoer before it gets to the target crossing point, as you should, you'll hardly have to move your barrel to the incomer. This width of stance, a shade wider than my trap stance, is right for me. Tall or short shooters should modify it for their own comfort.

expect to see the target. As soon as you see the target
sitting on the end of the gun, pull the trigger. Do not
look away until you see the target break. Do not move
until you see the second target cross the end of the gun.
Then swing, catch the bird, and shoot right at it. Be
sure to keep your cheek on the comb, and don't pull
your head up. Do not start your swing on the second
bird until you see it cross the barrel. Otherwise, you
may find yourself sitting back, waiting for the target
to come to you. On the second target, your swing is so
fast that it's possible to shoot right at the front of the
bird and the lead will be correct. You need not lead
the incomer on doubles as you did on singles for the
simple reason that you are swinging faster.

WHY YOU MISS STATION 1 DOUBLES

Experienced shooters miss here because they are not
ready. They fail to hold the muzzle just at the flight
line, holding either too high or too low. They shoot
entirely too fast, or look away when the trigger is
pulled. Beginners miss because of a lack of experience
on doubles, poor position, riding the first target out
too far, or looking up on the second target.

HOW TO HIT STATION 2 DOUBLES

You must remember that on all four double shots,
the first target is a non-recovery target. Your first move
must be correct. It is impossible on High 2 and Low 6
to change your mind once your swing has been started.

To shoot Station 2 doubles correctly, again concentrate on the first target as a single. Take exactly the
same position as you did on the High 2 single, facing
the target crossing point. Being sure to keep your right
leg straight, pivot back on the left leg, the weight on

the ball of the left foot. Your correct hold position should be at right angles to the flight line of the target. Keep the muzzle of the gun just below the chute opening, your eyes focused at infinity over the end of the barrel. Be sure you're ready and then give a good call. Do not move until you see the target. Once you see it, start your swing with the left arm, while pushing down with the right leg. As soon as you see daylight, pull the trigger. Do not move on the second target until you see it cross the barrel. This will usually have happened by the time you shoot the first target. Swing back, catch the second bird, and shoot right at it. Let both birds sit on top of the muzzle and follow through with your swing after you have fired. Do not look up after the first bird or after the second. Keep your eyes focused on the end of the barrel and the target at all times. The first target should be broken before it reaches the target crossing point. The second target should be broken about halfway between the crossing point and the high house.

An easy habit to get into is taking the second bird too much for granted and walking away before the shot is finished. Keep both feet planted on the ground and shoot the target.

WHY YOU MISS STATION 2 DOUBLES

The high house target is missed primarily by good shooters who fail to get ready, who try to shoot the target too fast, who take a poor position by keying around and facing the house too much thereby binding the swing, or who start their swing before the target has been seen. Inexperienced shooters ride the first target too far, swing back too fast on the second target, having to wait on it, have poor position and stance, or are afraid of the target and just give up.

HOW TO HIT STATION 6 DOUBLES

The first thing to do at Station 6 is to take a deep breath and pull yourself together. The fact that you haven't missed till now and have only two more stations to go is apt to make you tighten up. Pressure can make you do some strange things, like shooting out of turn, loading only one shell, or giving a squeaky call, and each of them can cost you a target. On the other hand, don't take the second target for granted. I have actually seen top shooters with one foot off the ground shooting at the second bird. Needless to say, this just doesn't work. Good concentration has taken you this far, so don't let up now.

To shoot Station 6 doubles, again treat the first target like a single bird. Take a position exactly facing the target crossing point. Mount your gun at shoulder level. Do not point it up in the sky. Swing back to your hold position, which is a shade less than a right angle to the flight line of the target. Be sure the muzzle is just below the flight line. Keep your line of sight over the end of the gun, out at infinity where you expect to see the target. Do not look at the trap opening unless you are a sustained-leader. Set yourself and give a good call. A good call at this point will instill confidence in your shooting.

Under no circumstances should you move on this target until you see it. Once you see it, pull the gun with the left hand, catch the target quickly, see daylight, pull the trigger, and follow through. Make sure you lean into the shot and do not straighten up with the swing. This will result in shooting over the target.

Once you've shot the first target, do not move on the second one until you see it cross the end of your gun. Swing back and catch it, pivoting on the left leg; this time see six to eight inches of daylight, and pull the trigger. This is a left-to-right shot on which your left arm will be trying to pull the gun back and your head up. Therefore, you must allow a little more lead than you did on the incomer at 2, though it is actually possible to hit the second target by shooting right at the leading edge of it if you continue your swing. Pivot on the left leg and do not walk away until you see the second target fully broken. The first target (outgoer) should be broken before it reaches the target crossing point. The second target should be shot halfway between the target crossing stake and the low house. Do not ride the second target too far as you will find your left arm pulling your head off the gun.

WHY YOU MISS STATION 6 DOUBLES

The commonest reason is nerves. But many shooters handicap themselves by facing the low house too much, and forgetting to swing through on the first bird; they try to snap it with a stationary gun in order to get on the second target more quickly. You don't have to hurry this much. Remember, you *want* the second target to come to you, and you've got to give it time to do so.

HOW TO HIT STATION 7 DOUBLES

Well, here you are at the last station. The only thing that can cause a miss here is a lack of concentration, but it happens a lot more often than you think. I have seen several world championships and world records lost on this station. After seeing Ben DiIorio miss on this station, costing him and Alex Kerr the long-run, two-man team .410 record, and then seeing D. Lee Braun miss on the same station, losing out on 100 straight with a .410, I thought that I had learned my lesson. But overconfidence is a sly mistress. It was not until I missed 100 straight on the same station by trying to shoot the first target too fast that I learned my lesson. Experience may be a hard teacher but it is a good one. I never step up to shoot this double that I don't remember that shot. I have never missed it again, but I'm knocking on wood as I say it.

To shoot Station 7 doubles correctly, take the same position as for a low house single. Point the gun directly over the target crossing stake. After all, that's where the target is supposed to go, so why hold to the left or the right? Be sure you have the muzzle of the gun as near as possible to the flight line of the target. Keep your eyes focused over the end of the gun out to where you expect to first see the target. Set yourself and give a good call. When the target comes out, take a good look at it. Be sure where it is going. Point the gun. Let the target sit on top of the barrel. Pull the trigger and follow through. Do not swing on the second target until it has crossed the barrel. Pick it up quickly. Follow it in. See daylight and pull the trigger. Keep your head firmly on the gun. Do not shift your eyes from the end of the gun and the target.

Try not to shoot the first target too fast, for this will break up your timing, giving you too much time to shoot the incomer. Usually, this results in swinging too far ahead, stopping the gun, and waiting and shooting behind the target. Remember to pivot on the left leg and keep the follow-through with the left arm, as this is a left-to-right shot which requires a little extra follow-through.

WHY YOU MISS STATION 7 DOUBLES

The main reasons for misses on this pair are: Shooting the first bird too fast; not being ready when the call is given; swinging back too fast and too far on the second target, and then having to spot-shoot it; and finally, not keeping the eyes focused on the end of the gun barrel and the target until the shot has been completed. Remember, the first bird is an outgoing target, a straightaway. Shoot promptly, but keep on looking at the target until the shot has been fired.

SHOOTING THE OPTIONAL

Now that you've broken all your doubles, it's *almost* time to congratulate you on your straight. All you've got to do is break your optional, which you must take at the Station 8 low house if you have not missed. Shoot it exactly as you did the preceding target. There's not the slightest difference. If you hit it once, you can hit it a hundred times if necessary. Just because it is the last shot in the round does not make it any more difficult. In fact, there is a lot less chance of missing this target than there is of missing High 7 or Low 7.

Before we leave the field, let me remind you that if you point at an object and ask ten shooters how far away it is, you'll get ten different answers. Thus, when I tell you the hold position for a stand, remember that it is what it looks like to me, as nearly as I can describe it. Look carefully at each picture, station by station, and try to get the feeling of where the gun is pointed. Also, refer to the diagrams of facing positions and hold positions. These diagrams are for pass shooting; shooters using sustained-lead always look at the target opening instead of in the vicinity of the gun barrel and always take a hold position farther from the house.

7

IMPROVING
YOUR SCORE

GO into any town in rural America and stop at the first hardware store, sporting goods store, or gas station you find. If there's a shotgun propped up in the corner and you mention duck hunting, it's an odds-on bet that someone will start bragging about an "Uncle Harry" or a "Bill Brown" or some other local character who can knock 'em down at sixty yards, catch 'em when they're crossing, and always kill a limit. And quite possibly he will be telling the truth.

Of course, if you take the time to check out his story, you'll probably find that Uncle Harry or Bill Brown is some old codger who got his start long before Ducks Unlimited existed, and still hunts four or five days a week even if it means closing the store.

What I am driving at is that to be a good shot, you've got to do a lot of shooting. If you want to shoot like Uncle Harry, you've got to get as much practice as he's had. You're not going to get it in the field. Uncle

The only real short-cut to timing and consistency is plenty of sound non-competitive practice at your home club, as much of it as you can afford. This attractive layout is part of the Outdoor Education Center of Yale University.

Harry and Bill started hunting in the days when the limit on ducks was determined by the number of shells you had in the blind. With today's limits, the shooting is usually over before you've had any real practice. Except on the skeet field.

In skeet, too, you can't expect to become a good shot unless you're prepared to put in your time and pop enough caps. Many pupils have asked me how much practice they should get, and to me that's like asking a hound dog how much you ought to hunt. His reply, if he could talk, would likely be, "Every chance you get," and I can't put it any better. For the only way you learn is through repetition. Do anything often enough, and the subconscious mind will take over and make it a habit. Do it correctly, and it becomes a good habit; do it wrong, and it becomes a bad habit.

If you can consciously replace your bad habits with good, or correct ones, they will gradually become subconscious reactions. Good habits release your conscious mind and let you concentrate on the competitive situation and the fine points of shooting. Thus, as good habits establish themselves, your shooting becomes easier and your scores improve more and more.

Let's face it, if you are only going to shoot half a dozen times a year, you can't hope to progress very far or become much of a skeet shot. So if you decide that you want to shoot skeet, take it seriously and join a club with a shooting program. It will further motivate you to shoot more regularly. For regular, consistent shooting is the first essential for improving your score.

Shooting one or two days a week may be all the time you can afford, and this is better than nothing. However, as a weekend shooter, it will often take you a couple of rounds to warm up and get in the groove. By then, the shooting is over and you are cold by the time you shoot the following weekend. When you shoot every day, picking up that groove after the first few rounds comes quicker and quicker.

Thus the best approach is to try to shoot several days a week, and then to periodically use a vacation period for an intensive effort, shooting every day for the week or ten days. If you can shoot near home, shoot evenings, but shoot regularly, the oftener back-to-back, the better. Intensive shooting, closely spaced, is far better for your score than the same amount of shooting scattered over several months or a year. And two or three intensive shooting periods a year are good even if you shoot on a regular but sparse schedule.

There are two basic kinds of practice shooting; remedial shooting, to correct a particular bad habit, and general non-competitive shooting aimed at developing timing and consistency.

Non-competitive shooting is a form of practice in which you relax and enjoy the shooting with your friends. You talk, are sociable, and are having fun. All you need do is watch the shooter's targets ahead of you and cut out the horse play when you step on that station. Then, you concentrate just as if you were in a tournament.

If you are a D, E, or beginning shooter, you need to do as much of this non-competitive, repetitive form of shooting as you can spare the time and money for, in order to establish sound habit patterns. In fact, as long as your misses are fairly evenly distributed among the eight stations, nothing more should be required to maintain a steady improvement in your scores.

If you are human, however, the chances are that you'll soon find certain shots predominating over others —say, High 2 or Low 5—and find that most of your misses are concentrated at a certain "difficult station" or stations. That's where remedial practice comes in. But let me tell you this: There is no such thing as a difficult station—it is the shooter who has the difficulty.

Usually, your difficult station is simply a station at which your technique is shaky, because you can't remember (or perhaps never knew) the best way to deal with it. Technical insecurity is quickly reflected in a loss of confidence, and wherever you lack confidence on the skeet field, that's where your difficult targets will be.

The real concern is that worry about a difficult target seldom stops there. Worrying about it makes you miss targets that you know how to hit, and thinking about that miss makes you drop yet another bird. Then you begin to doubt and wonder if there isn't something more basic wrong. You begin to hesitate and change your timing. You become so anxious to see whether or not you have broken the target that you begin lifting your eyes, and then your head. Before you know it, you are not only having trouble with difficult birds—you're getting to the point where you can't be sure of breaking anything, anywhere on the field.

In shotgun shooting, the more you miss the more you're apt to look away. But remember, the eye constitutes the back sight. So every time you raise your head to see if you've hit the target, you are raising the back sight and causing the gun to shoot over the top of the target.

Remedial practice is easy in skeet because of the fixed angle of flight of the birds. All you have to do is ask the trap boy to pull the house you wish, and shoot a box of shells from the station that's been troubling you. Of course, the cheapest form of remedial practice in the long run is to get first-class professional coaching. By the time you've given a few thousand lessons to experts as well as novices, you can spot things in seconds that would take the shooter hours of experimenting to uncover.

The reason for this is that the coach looks for the cause of the miss and not at the miss. What you need desperately is for someone to tell you *why* you are missing. Most of the shooters who try to help you only look at the target and tell you that you are behind or over. You could be behind the target for four or five reasons, and the why is what you need to know. Whether your left hand is out too far, or your right foot is behind the left foot, or you're stopping your gun. This is what a good coach can tell you and when he tells you, take his advice. Nine times out of ten, he knows what he's talking about.

Even when you know exactly what you are doing wrong, however, as a result of either self-analysis or outside help, it can still be a problem to correct it. Let me tell you a secret: The answer very often lies in redirecting your attention away from hitting the target and focusing it instead on what you are doing to hit

If you hit a bad slump, don't fool around too long with home-made remedies—the best place to get help is from a pro.

the target, that is, onto the movements that lead to the breaking of the bird.

Asking another shooter for advice is often a mistake, even if he can break a good score. The fact that he's worked hard enough to learn to score his way doesn't mean that his way is right for you, or even for him, for that matter. It just shows that he's put in his time.

On the whole, if you can't get professional coaching, you're probably better off trying to work out your own salvation with the help of a book such as this. You won't find too many shortcuts, but if you use your head, you should be able to avoid some of the detours.

If circumstances force you to be your own coach and shooting analyst, one thing that can help you to understand your misses is to learn how to interpret the targets you break. If you are right on, the target will be powdered. If a chip flies off the nose, you have probably been ahead of the target; if the larger part of a target skips above the flight line after you have broken it, you are holding the muzzle too low. If you chip the top of the bird, then you are above it and so on. How your chips fly will tell you where the bulk of your pattern is and indicate if you are using only the fringe of the pattern, or really centering your birds.

It's really important, if you are going to try to improve strictly on your own, to do it systematically and to take the time and effort to set up a specific program —if not on paper, then at least in your mind. This is an important step in the scheme of improving. If you're coaching yourself, it's obvious that you'll have to do a lot of experimenting. But let me give you two bits of advice: First, experiment with only one thing at a time. Otherwise, you'll never be able to figure out what your experiments are proving.

And secondly, don't be in too much of a hurry to change guns. If you shot good scores with your gun last year, there's no reason why you cannot shoot good scores with it this year. Indiscriminate gun changing can lead only to one thing, and that is trouble. (Most of the time, double trouble.) Never pass judgment on a borrowed gun until you have shot six rounds with it. Most borrowed guns feel good for a round or two; you shoot better simply because a strange gun forces you to return to fundamentals in order to shoot it. About the third round, you begin to miss the same target you were missing with your own gun, plus a few extras. Of all the things that can go wrong with your shooting, I would say that gun trouble would be the least of the lot. Guns do not change. Shooters do. Before you change guns, go look into the mirror. Ask yourself,

"What am I doing wrong?" Then go out and try to correct it.

In the long run, your solution will always lie in going back to the fundamentals and concentrating on them, especially on the positive act that corrects the flaw that has been working its way into your form. Take the time to run down the entire list of basics—stance, position, gunmounting, holding points—and make certain that none of these basics has gone awry. Nine times out of ten one of them has, and nine times out of ten that's what you eventually pay the coach for hammering back into your skull.

Trying "to shoot your way out" is the worst thing you can do when you find yourself in a slump. You are blindly continuing and wastefully hoping that something will change. This is often the first effort that a novice shooter tries, and it's about the last thing that ever works. The next thing is that he usually tries some gimmick, one with some unorthodox wrinkle. This will lead him in a direction exactly opposite to the way he should be heading. When you're having trouble, concentrate on fundamentals and try to come back to a style that is more orthodox, not less.

Whether you're averaging in the 70's or 90's, you can console yourself with the thought that *nobody* ever got so good that he didn't have to watch out for little tell-tale signs that he was slipping. In fact, one of the biggest problems in skeet is that even top shooters have a tendency to fall into small bad habits. For instance, I shoot a dismounted gun. If I am not careful, I find myself dropping the stock lower and lower until finally it reaches a point of no return and causes a miss. The big trouble with these habits is that you are not conscious of them yourself. Everything feels right and you think you are doing everything right except that you're just not centering the target, or perhaps not hitting it as easily as you used to.

The three commonest bad habits that AA shooters fall into are as follows: First, they have a tendency to keep creeping around more and more toward the target opening, trying to shoot the target faster and faster. They are not aware that by swinging around farther toward the target opening they are binding their swing and using their arms instead of the whole body to complete the shot. Because only a few targets get away, they do not realize that they are making a vital mistake. The targets they do hit look so good that they can't believe that they are doing something to create the misses.

Secondly, they start moving their hold position farther and farther out in front of the chute. The thought is that they will catch the target sooner and be able to break it sooner. This is just the opposite to what happens. By holding farther in front of the chute, you cut your swing in half, because you must wait longer to start your swing.

A third common error of good shooters is to get over-anxious and start the muzzle of the gun moving before they have really seen the target. This is a bad habit that is encouraged by the instant pull, but that's no excuse for bad shooting. Train yourself to wait until you see the target. If you start the gun moving before that, your gun will arrive where you want to shoot the bird before the bird gets there. Therefore, you must stop and wait on it, not realizing that even though the apparent lead was correct when you pulled the trigger, your gun had stopped.

So, if you're having trouble on High 2 or Low .6, check these three things. Remember, once you have established your hold position, there is no reason to change it from one year to the next. I have been shooting since 1939, and I still use the same hold position that I used then, and I still break just as good scores, if not better. Just because you become a few years older doesn't mean that you have to hold farther out in front of the target opening in order to maintain proper lead. Your reaction time doesn't slow down that much.

Another common bad habit is unconsciously picking up someone else's timing, whether too fast or too slow. If you often shoot with a squad of shooters who shoot their targets fast, without knowing it you will begin to pick up their timing. Sometimes this works out to your advantage and you shoot better. But most of the time, you find you begin missing and cannot understand why.

No discussion of problems can ignore the subject of flinching, for this is something that can afflict novices and good shooters alike. I'm not sure that it's quite as common as many people suppose, however, for it has been my observation that there are very few true flinchers among experienced shooters. The true flincher is someone who is afraid of the gun, or more accurately, afraid of recoil, and we will discuss his plight in a minute. Most apparent flinching, however, is of psychological rather than physical origin, and is caused by indecision in the shooter's mind as to when to pull the trigger. The shooter becomes so afraid that he may not hit the target that he fails to pull, hoping to make sure, hoping to wait a little longer and get to where he will be certain to hit the target. By doing this, he accomplishes the very thing that he is trying to avoid, a miss. This fault can be caused by too much shooting with the .410 gun. This type of flinching is purely psychological and can readily be overcome.

Sometimes riding an incomer too far, such as on a windy day, can cause a flinch. Once you have passed that moment of truth where you should have pulled the trigger, anything can happen. The longer you look at the target, the more you are apt to jerk your head up and also jerk the trigger.

Let me give you a tip. If you have been having trouble with flinching, when you take your hold position, and are ready to call for the bird, the last thing you tell yourself is to *look for the target*. If you concentrate on looking for the target, you will forget to flinch.

Unlike apparent flinching, true flinching is caused by fear of recoil. The shooter begins to anticipate the pounding of the gun and draws back from it, in an involuntary reaction involving the body, finger, and trigger of the gun. You may not think that recoil is the problem, and outwardly may have no fear of it. But since flinching is a subconscious reaction, an instinctive reaction of the body to protect itself from harm, the shooter has little control of it.

The body action caused by true flinching is a jerking movement that includes the trigger finger and the head. Movement after the gun is fired cannot affect the accuracy of the shot, but in most instances the flinch precedes the shot by a split second, and a miss results.

If you think that you may have started flinching, the first solutions to look for are physical ones. Check your gun fit, especially if you shoot with a dropped stock, and make sure that the butt stock is seating properly in your shoulder pocket. If your gun fit is correct, but you still get too much recoil, shift to a heavier gun, or to an autoloader if you aren't already using one. Or shift down to a 20-gauge for a few rounds.

A final physical factor to consider is trigger pull. Most factory triggers fall in the four- to six-pound range, but every now and then a real heavy one slips through. Personally, I prefer pulls between three and five pounds. If you think your trigger pull is too hard or too creepy, get a good gunsmith to adjust it for you. But whatever you do, don't go to a hair trigger. These can cause safety problems that are a whole lot harder to deal with than flinching.

Finally, there are two bad habits that are very easy to correct. One is putting the left arm too far out on the forearm, the other is "stock crawling". I have seen shooters who, without knowing it, kept pushing their left hand farther and farther out on the forearm until finally they had their finger over the magazine cap. When I pointed out their mistake to them, most of them didn't even realize that they were doing it. The same thing is true of creeping up the stock. By creeping, I mean shoving the head further and further up the comb. Stock crawlers finally wind up with their nose almost touching the back of their thumb. This not only destroys the correct sight picture but also binds the neck muscles, causing the head to come up off the stock when a left-to-right angle shot is made.

These are just a few of the bad habits that are so easy to acquire. I have never understood why it takes so *much* practice to create good habits while bad habits seem to entrench themselves without any invitation. But I guess that's life.

8

TOURNAMENT SKEET

PHYSICALLY, tournaments aren't much different from the practice rounds of skeet you shoot on your home field. The targets fly about the same way, and you use the same gun and ammo and hopefully the same smooth shooting technique. As much as 90 percent of the factors involved in shooting a good tournament score are physical factors, and that helps, because it's usually possible to control most physical factors, and eliminate those that might make you fail.

So far, most of this book has been devoted to physical factors—to the choice and fit of equipment and the mechanics of sound shooting technique. So by now, you ought to have a pretty good grasp of 90 percent of the factors that make up tournament success. The trouble is, getting control over physical factors just puts you on about the same level as all the other serious shooters. Most of the tournament competitors at any shoot use approximately equivalent equipment and shooting techniques. Any edge you gain on them physically will be a narrow one. (Of course, that doesn't mean you don't take those little edges, too.)

In the end result, then, the factors that make up the remaining 10 percent of tournament success often make all the difference. And these factors are largely psychological rather than physical. It's like most competitive sports, and even business situations: you try to get control of all the physical factors and eliminate as far as possible every chance of a physical mistake so that you can concentrate on the fine points.

In other words, winning is usually a case of striving for perfection yourself, and letting your opponent make the mistakes. This is especially true in skeet, for in skeet your success in defeating the other shooters is a by-product of your success against the targets.

The main psychological difference between shooting at home and tournament shooting is that in the tournament every shot *counts*—you know that every miss is for record, and even a single one can put you out of the race. This knowledge can paralyze you if you let it, but it can also help if you learn to channel your excitement and put it to work for you. Hopefully, there will be some degree of emotional tension in every tournament you ever enter. Yes, I mean hopefully—it's got to be there, no matter how many tournaments you've shot in. Show me a shooter who can't get keyed up for a tournament, and I'll beat him every day in the week. For getting keyed up is the key to concentration, as long as you stay physically relaxed at the same time. Actually, that's all that concentration is—getting keyed up mentally while staying relaxed physically—and thus the ability to get keyed up is very close to having the will to win, or *desire*, as they call it these days.

I can give a shooter everything else he needs to win, but the desire has to come from him. It may be only a

When a striped-shirted referee replaces the familiar trap boy and the scoring is for keeps, many shooters find that skeet becomes "a whole nother ball game." But hang in there, for the only way to win tournaments is to shoot in tournaments.

Note that although all four shooters have their guns resting on their feet, the actions are open and the guns are perfectly safe.

spark that needs kindling, but the spark has to be there. If you have no real desire to compete, then forget about tournament shooting, for without a will to win you'll be licked no matter how well you learn to dominate the physical factors. But don't give in too early. Don't go to a tournament or two, shoot badly, figure you just can't handle the pressure, and quit in disgust.

There is only one way to control pressure, and it works like this, once your basic technique is sound: The

more confidence you have, the more targets you break:
the more targets you break, the easier it becomes; and
the easier it becomes, the more confidence you have.
Now that we've got that out of the way, let's look at
some of the incidental factors that have a big bearing
on tournament success.

START AT THE BEGINNING

Through a combination of skill and dumb luck (I
won't say in what proportion) I managed to start at the
top in tournament skeet and still survive. The very first
tournament I ever entered was the Nationals, and I won
the professional class. (They call it the industry class
now, but that's another story.) I don't recommend this
procedure at all. In fact, the main advice I'd like to
give the novice shooter is, "Start at the beginning and
don't get greedy."

The way to learn to shoot is to shoot, and the way to
win tournaments is to shoot in tournaments. I don't
care how many 100 straights you break at home—shooting at a tournament for the first time is going to affect
the way you shoot and how well you shoot.

Let's say you've gotten to where you can run straight
at home, and decide to enter your first state shoot.
Quite possibly you'll find it difficult to relax and swing
easily, and thus you'll drop more birds than you would
at home. But next year, if you go to the state shoot
again, you're more than likely to shoot the way you
do at home. Take on a regional shoot, and you'll probably perform there as you did at your first state shoot.
But if you come back again, you'll do better. Finally,
you try the Nationals and you botch it again. But state
and regional shoots are now old hat to you, and if you
stick with it, the Nationals will be, too. No matter how

good you are, these first attempts we've been talking about do something to you.

Having just finished saying that confidence is important to the tournament shooter, I can't very well advise you to "think small" when you start out, and I sure don't want to discourage you from believing in yourself. But I do want you to think realistically. I've known beginners who entered their first tournament expecting to be high over-all at the end of the day and ended up not even winning their own class. Let's face it, if you are a beginner or a D or C shooter, you have no business thinking you can outshoot the AA hot-shots. Concentrate on winning your own class and moving up to the next. Don't worry about knocking off the big boys until you've reached Class A yourself. They'll still be there.

SQUADDING

Here's another tip for the novice tournament shooter: Try to avoid being placed on the lead-off position on a squad. Instead, try to shoot 2nd, 3rd, or 4th. By the same token, don't shoot 5th, or last. Even the best-meaning squads sometimes forget and aren't as courteous as they should be. They walk to the next station leaving the 5th man behind. Too often, he'll find himself rushed, and being hurried puts you at a disadvantage. I know—it's happened to me, and I try not to shoot last if I can avoid it. But if I'm stuck there, I don't make too much of it. While I take my time, I don't try to take too much time.

Weather and time of day are other things that can affect your shooting. Of course, to be a good shooter, you have to learn how to compensate for and discipline yourself under all conditions. However, I do not take this to mean that you shouldn't try to eliminate as many other variables as possible when you get up to shoot, if it will make shooting easier for you. For instance, after shooting in a few tournaments, if you find after a while that you can shoot better at a certain time of day, then do it. Try to squad up at that time. Just don't let it become an obsession. You should be able to shoot at any time of the day. But, if you like to shoot in the morning, you are certainly going to shoot better at that time. So, make every effort to squad up at the time you think is best for you.

It's best not to go to a shoot and try to adjust your shooting time according to what the local weather conditions are at that time of day. You should be able to shoot under any conditions. The best you can do most of the time is to learn how to handle the wind and hope that it proves pretty much the same for everybody.

Another variable you can control is the way you take your misses. Just as there is a right way to hit a target, there is also the right way to miss one. What happens is that you're going great with a long run and no misses. Because of some minor distraction, you lose your concentration and drop a bird. Then you really blow it. You drop the next one, and the next one, and sometimes more; it may take several birds before you re-establish your concentration. You are so upset because you are not going to break a perfect score, thinking that this is what it takes to win, that you lose your concentration momentarily.

Remember, any score can win a tournament. I have seen the World Championship in .410 won with a 95, and the shoot-off in the same event with a 21. I found out early in the game that it was not the first miss after the shoot was over that bugged me, but the second. This was the one that cost me the runner-up trophy, which I threw away by missing some simple, easy targets simply because I had missed a hard one to start with.

Let me give you a good illustration. In the World Championship in Savannah, I had a long run of 200. All the other pros had missed either in the first 100 or the second 100. I had second place in the tournament sewed up with a long run of 200. In the first 25 of the last 50, however, I dropped a Low 5. I was so disappointed that momentarily I lost my concentration, walked over, and missed a Low 6. In a matter of minutes, I had not only thrown away the championship, but also the second place that I would have taken with a long run of 249. The 248 didn't even take sixth place. So, when you miss a target, stop, take a deep breath, relax for a moment, and perhaps take a step backward. Then, assume the correct position again. Do not let your emotions cost you a target. However, do not overdo it. Too much worrying or fidgeting can extend the lost bird run. When you get into the correct position, don't wait too long before you call for the bird. But, don't call for it until you are sure you are ready. Then let your habitual shooting habits take over. Rely on your reflexes. If you've learned properly, you'll see the bird powder.

Along the same lines, broken targets or for that matter any interruptions in the round have their effect on your shooting. The reasons why the targets are broken aren't important, but the no-bird throw can have its effect on the psychology of your shooting. It interrupts your concentration.

INTERPRETING THE RULES

The old gentleman who taught me how to shoot used to say that if the target is more than three feet off the ground, shoot it. And if you didn't bust your bird right in the middle and splatter it into a hundred pieces, you shouldn't argue about it. I've found that these two pieces of advice have always worked for me because they leave me with a free mind, and keep me from trying to talk myself into something I didn't deserve. By the time you argue with the referee, you've usually upset yourself and broken the timing of your squad as well, and you often have a tendency to miss the next bird anyway. Don't make problems for yourself. If there is a flagrant infraction of a rule, you are entitled to protest; but don't call chips pieces and try and talk yourself into thinking you got more of the bird than you deserved.

Remember that the rule book states you have the right to refuse an irregular target, but it is up to the referee, and to him alone, as to whether or not the target was irregular. So my advice to you is to shoot a wayward target unless it is so erratic that anyone who saw it could also tell. If it is only slightly out of line, the best thing you can do is shoot it because the referee can say it wasn't and you've lost. It is always his word against yours.

An illegal target—one that doesn't go the required distance—is something different. Very seldom do you see an illegal target, but you do see a lot of irregular targets. Actually, very few shooters really are aware of how much a target can deviate, according to the rule book, and still be legal. There exists a good three-foot radius over the crossing point through which it may fly. On the other end is a 55-yard marker and an interpretation of the rule doesn't have anything to do with the 55-yard marker because the target doesn't have to hit the marker. It can hit ten feet to the left or right. People have grown into the habit of watching the target come out of the chute on either Station 1 or 7, look at it as it crosses the target crossing point, and feel that it must land on the marker 55 yards away. That just ain't so.

If you do get a broken target on a station that's already tough for you, the main thing you have to overcome is the "why did this have to happen to me *here?*" feeling. Tell yourself that you have broken it before a hundred times, so that there is no reason why you can't break it again, just because one target comes out broken. The same thing happens to everybody. You should lower your gun, take a deep breath, reset yourself, go through your same old motions, and then call for the target. You are taking too much of a chance to stand there with the gun ready, waiting for the target.

Let me put it this way: You build yourself up to a point on every shot, and when you call for the bird you have reached the height of that point. Any time after that, if you don't shoot, it will be downhill, and you are apt to miss the target. On the other hand, do not make a big production of this as I have seen some people do.

TWO THINGS A BEGINNER MUST LEARN

First, you must learn not to count targets. Otherwise, the longer the run, the more pressure you will be putting on your shooting ability. When I first started shooting, I must have shot twenty 24's before I finally shot a straight, simply because I kept counting targets, looking for that last shot. To some shooters the first straight comes easily. To others, it takes time. But it can be done; it simply takes concentration.

I have never liked the theory of concentrating on each target singly. To me, this builds too much pressure on the shooter. I would much prefer to concentrate on each round. There are only four rounds. There are a hundred targets. Try convincing yourself that all skeet ranges are the same. The targets thrown here will be the same as the ones thrown at your home range, where you break them all every time. Everyone has to shoot the same targets. No one can break more than 100. All you have to do is break four 25's, which you do every day at home. So, go out and break them one at a time. Convince yourself that you are just going out to practice. Try taking a little breather, say five or ten minutes, between each round. Do not make the referee have to call you. A slight break between rounds has always helped me ease the pressure.

By breaking the event down into four 25's, you eliminate that magic number of 100, which all too often causes you to miss one target here or there. If you do miss a target, tell yourself right then and there that you've started working on another long run and intend to break the world's record. You have to miss sometime, just try and put it off as long as possible. There's not actually any difference between the first target and the last target in a run of one thousand. They're both the same size. They both fly the same speed and fly in the same direction. If you break the first one, you should be able to break the last one. Fear of missing is the greatest psychological block in shooting.

Looking at the score board is the same kind of thing. If it bothers you, by all means don't do it. On the other hand, some shooters, by knowing what they have to shoot, actually do better. Find out what you like to do, then act accordingly.

Another thing you must learn to do is not to let your competition bother you. By this I mean that you should not give up as soon as you see Joe Blow or John Henry, who are top AA shooters, walk on the ground. It takes a little time to get over this. In fact, some shooters never get over it. I can remember when Dick Shaughnessy, Grant Ilseng, or Alex Kerr walked on the grounds. Half of the shooters would give up before firing a shot. You must convince yourself that they are no better than you

Score-board watching is all right if it helps your concentration to know what you have to do. Otherwise, you're better off to wait until your rounds are history to see where you stand.

are. They can only break a 100, and after all, you have broken a 100 yourself. Go out and break your 100 and then sit back and see if they can tie it. This is true in any sport. There's plenty of room for an upset, and new hot-shots are always appearing on the scene to take over from the old champions.

Be content to work your way up to the top. But once you are there, keep telling yourself that you are just as good as the boys who are there—otherwise you wouldn't be there. Once you reach the top, it's a simple story: The shooter who concentrates the most at a particular shoot is the one who comes out with the top score. You are not going to win them all; just try to win more than the other fellow.

AVERAGE CARDS

If you attend a lot of shoots, your average card probably looks a lot like your report card when you were in the 7th grade. I have always felt that average cards were a necessary evil—*necessary* because it is the only true way we have of knowing a shooter's ability, and *evil* because all too often shooters begin to worship the card as if it controlled the shooter instead of merely reflecting the shooter's ability. It begins to have adverse psychological effects on a shooter's thinking and can undermine his confidence.

The first effects of the average-card obsession become apparent when a shooter begins withdrawing from tournaments because of bad weather. He's afraid that a little wind or rain, or even cold will hamper his ability to shoot his best. He's afraid he will come up with a lower score and his average will reflect this in the card. Next, he will stop going to certain clubs where tournaments are held because of its background or other immediate shooting conditions. Finally, he will reach the point where he is afraid to pull the trigger at that "moment of truth" that is so necessary in shotgun shooting. He rides his targets a little farther, trying to make sure it will be a hit, only to miss. He is doing the very thing he is trying to avoid.

Keep in mind that the only reason for a tournament is to establish the best shot. If you shoot only under perfect conditions, you haven't proved a thing. Tom, Dick, and Harry may be able to outshoot you every time under these conditions. Unless you try them under every type of condition, you cannot be sure that they are better than you. You may be able to take them on a windy, rainy day.

You should shoot for two reasons—first, just for the enjoyment of shooting, and second, to win. And they should stay in that order. As soon as winning becomes more important than the fun of shooting, you will find it more and more difficult to win simply because you cannot relax. Someone must lose or there wouldn't be a winner. Your goal should be just to try to win more often than the other fellow.

If you enjoy shooting, you will shoot better, so by all means do everything that will make it easier for you to win. You can do this by picking a good squad or shooting with friends if possible. Try to squad with better shooters. Go to the shoots where you have the best time, both on and off the field. All this makes shooting a lot more fun, and good scores will come a lot easier because of a better balanced psychological approach to the sport.

However, if the weather does turn bad after you arrive, or if the State Shoot is at a club with a rough background, do not stay home just to protect your average. It is possible to win with any score. You may pull down your average, but you won, and that is the whole point. You could stay home and protect your 99 average, but what good is an average? You can't put it in a show case. I haven't seen very many average cards framed. Deep down inside, you even have a little guilty feeling because you know it is not a completely true average.

Your average card is just a portable file cabinet. If your average goes down, it shows that you need practice. If you go to a shoot, it verifies the class in which you say you are supposed to shoot. Keep it that way. Shoot your best, whatever the conditions, and your average will take care of itself.

I would rather be pointed out as the shooter who won the Great Eastern in a 30-mile-an-hour wind with a 95, than as a shooter with a 99-plus average who stayed home.

PRACTICE ROUNDS

Practice rounds can build you up psychologically when you are going to shoot for record—but only if you treat them strictly as practice. You should always shoot to break targets, and thus shoot seriously. But if you miss during a practice round, you must realize that you weren't primed mentally to break them all—you were simply loosening your muscles, getting ready for the record shoot. Don't let your practice round score affect the way you shoot in competition.

When you get to the shooting grounds, you should know how much practice it takes to get you primed for the main event. Personally, I don't like to shoot more than one box of shells before competing. All I need to do is to get the feel of the gun and the pull of the trigger. So, I spread the shots around on those targets which I feel will help get my tempo in line, such as High 1, 2, and 3, and Low 5 and 6. As soon as I'm hitting these targets well, I quit, even if I have shells left in my pocket. I know that once I feel right, there's no use shooting anymore. I'm only risking the chance of losing confidence by missing two or three shots at one particular bird. Others feel they need more practice than that. If it takes you three or four rounds to get keyed up and ready to shoot, by all means go to the practice range and take whatever time you need.

Some shooters, however, seem to go to the shoot just to practice. They're constantly on the practice range, before the event and after the event. They remind me of a bird dog I once had. As soon as the car was stopped, he would jump out of the car and run up and down the road the whole time I was getting out my hunting coat, shells, and gun. By the time I was ready to start hunting, he was so pooped he couldn't even jump the fence. If you want to go to a shoot just to shoot, all well and good. But if you want to go to a shoot to win, then I suggest you not waste all your efforts on the practice range. Learn how to shoot at home. You should practice just enough to sharpen yourself up to do what you have learned before you came to the shoot. Too much practice can be just as damaging as too little.

SHOOT-OFFS

Let's imagine that one day you finally do everything right and you post four 25's on the tournament scoreboard. Not too long ago, if you broke them all, like this, you could pick up the trophy, smile at the birdie, and go home. But today, we have more good shooters than ever before, and you may very well find yourself tied with a bunch of hotshots who have also broken 100. A tie means just one thing—a shoot-off.

So what? If you've got the right psychological approach, shoot-offs are no more difficult than the main event. In fact, I've always told myself that they were actually easier for the simple reason that once you've made the shoot-off, you no longer have to outshoot several hundred other shooters, only the three or four who have made it to the shoot-off. You wouldn't be tied with them if you weren't just as good as they are. You are all going to shoot the same stations and targets, so all you need do is keep doing the right things until the others make a mistake, and be ready to accept their congratulations.

Being ready to do your best in a shoot-off isn't much different from being ready for another round. Be sure your equipment is ready well in advance, and remember to include your clear glasses—shoot-offs start late and end later. If you shot in an early squad, break a few practice targets half an hour or so before the last squad finishes, just to get that feeling again, but remember to treat it as a practice round. Also, wind and weather conditions may have changed since you shot the 100, and the practice round will tell you how much.

DOUBLES AT ALL STATIONS

In my estimation, doubles at all stations is another necessary evil of modern-day skeet tournaments, the only practicable way to eliminate long shoot-offs. I don't mind long shoot-offs—in fact, I enjoy them—and some of my best memories are coupled with them. But club management often wants to get the shoot over, especially if it is late in the day or late in the season, where there is a possibility of shooting without light.

In principle, doubles at all stations is rather unfair. It's like saying in trap, "well, we have tied at 16-yard singles, so let's go to handicap and see who is the best man." The man who wins won't be the 16-yard champ as much as the handicap champ, for the latter has little to do with the former.

Doubles at all stations is a completely different game. I consider myself a fairly good field shot, and this has given me experience in widely varied kinds of shooting. If you made me shoot doubles at all stations against Tom, Dick, and Harry, who are school shooters, shooters who shoot each station by the numbers, I think I could outshoot them. Not because I might be a better shot—but because my experience in a variety of shooting in the field would give me an edge on doubles at Stations 3, 4, and 5. This would be true unless they had been practicing doubles at all stations.

This brings up a point. If you are an A, AA, or AAA shooter, I'd advise you to practice doubles at all stations. If you're not, don't be like the D shooter who once came to me for a lesson. "Now," he said, after we had finished, "I'd like to spend tomorrow shooting

doubles at all stations." I asked why. He said he thought
he might now get into a shoot-off. "First, you have to
get to the shoot-off," I replied, "and that's a long way
off." All class winners are determined by long runs,
and only championships are run with doubles at all
stations. You've got to keep the horse before the cart.
He hadn't thought of that.

The problem of doubles at all stations is not so much
one of physical difficulty but a psychological one. If
you take the time to stop and think about it, you shoot
Stations 1, 2, 6, and 7 as doubles. At Stations 3, 4, and
5, you must approach them as if you were shooting
singles. Remember when you broke into shooting doubles at 1 and 2, and 6 and 7? You were told to shoot
for the first bird in a pair, taking it like a single, and
then go after the second bird. The approach to Stations
3, 4, and 5 is exactly the same. You have ample time
to break the first target and enough left over to get the
second without getting upset. I will admit that Station
4 does become a challenge, but it can be mastered.

No matter how or what you say, shooters still panic
at the mention of doubles at all stations. The reason for
this is inexperience which breeds a lack of confidence.
If you will take the time in practice to erase the un-
familiarity with these three stations, you will have an
edge on the competition during a shoot-off.

The shooter who missed at 3 and the other stations
is psyched out. He is apt to miss even at Stations 1 and
2 when he is in a doubles shoot-off. He has been telling
himself that he must shoot doubles all the way around,
and this interrupts his thinking and confidence on the
first two stations. If he does get by 1 and 2, then he is
stopped at 3 because he thinks the birds are moving
faster and he must swing faster. By now you know that
swinging too fast will put you ahead of the target and
you must wait for the bird. Once you stop that gun you

are about as good as lost because the target passes you by.

If our novice doubles shooter had taken the shoot-off as a normal round, with the first bird just like a singles bird, he would have done much better. After all, if you drop that first bird, what good is the second? It probably has put you out of the winning.

Station 4 is another psych-out station for most shooters because they see the bird whizzing across the field so fast, even though they know it's just the angle that makes it appear that way. After all, you did shoot it from both houses as singles, so why can't you shoot it as doubles? If you've come this far in skeet shooting, you must know that there is plenty of time, so why rush?

And rush is what you do if you do it wrong. Too fast a swing will make you stop the gun. Most shooters try to get on the first bird fast, so that they can have more time on the second bird, or so they can break it before it gets out of the pattern. But this means that they will make a too-short swing on the first bird, and this then cuts down on their swing for the second bird. What is even worse, even if you do swing short and hit the first bird, you don't realize that you were even shorter on the second when you missed it. It's the half-swing that misses the second birds on 4 as well as the two targets on either side station.

The correct way to shoot Station 4 is to shoot the first bird as if it were a single target and follow through with the swing after you have shot, which will carry you past the target crossing point. Then, swing back and shoot right *at* the second target. Don't lead that second target. If you didn't stop your swing on the first bird, the swing after the second will be ample to take care of the lead and allow you to shoot directly at the target. Shooters who have not practiced doubles at all stations will miss the second bird on 4 because they try to lead the bird. They usually stop the swing short on the first target, then jump to the second, get three feet ahead on the second, and stop there and miss.

So, if you shoot the first bird as a normal shot, then your full swing will take you back faster on the second bird, which you can shoot as soon as you are on it. Your gun will break the target clean, well before the boundary line. There is no advantage trying to shoot the bird right over the center, and even though that immediate pow-pow might sound good, it doesn't always break two targets.

Sometimes a question arises when shooting doubles at all stations as to which bird to take first. From 1 through 4, always shoot the high house bird first if you are right-handed. The opposite is true for left-handed shooters. This takes into account the natural direction of your swing which works best on the low house. You save your better swing for the second bird.

A few shooters can't shoot Station 4 well by taking the high house first. By all means, they should take the low house first if it is easier. You can take the birds any way you want on doubles, just as long as you tell the referee before you shoot.

On Stations 5, 6, and 7, you shoot the low house first because it is the faster target, and the outgoer.

HANDLOADS

Handloading is a big thing these days in all shotgun shooting sports, from the field to the range. Because of the costs a shooter must bear, handloads are now allowed at most registered meets. A club can hold longer programs and give better trophies while shooters can shoot more for less. Handloads can keep the cost of skeet shooting within the grasps of the general public. About the only shoot I know of where handloads aren't allowed is at the Nationals. Here, the reason is based on time saved rather than any fear of possible dishonesty.

Personally, I do not have the time to handload. If I did, however, I would shoot handloads in practice and small shoots. But if I went to a state or regional tournament, where a lot is at stake, I would prefer the confidence of shooting factory ammunition. I don't think that there is much difference in the capability of the shells because of the efficiency of modern handloading equipment except in the matter of quality control. However, there is no handloader alive who can control the quality of shot-shell like the ammunition manufacturers.

Consequently, in a big or important tournament, I want to know that the ammunition I shoot is going to perform properly every time. It's one less physical factor to worry about. If you have ever had a blooper in your handloads, you will understand what I am talking about. The thought is always there, even if it never happens. I have seen everything from blown barrels to 200 straights shot with handloads. The difference is in the person doing the loading, not in the components. If you handload, do it with precision. See how perfect you can be, not how fast. Your fast loads may be your last loads.

Shooting the Smaller Gauges

Novice tournament shooters are not required to shoot all the gauges in a meet. You can shoot any gauge you wish but if you shoot anything but the 12, you're probably doing yourself more harm than good. I'm convinced that most lower class shooters should leave the little guns alone until they have mastered the 12-gauge. As soon as you have done so, however—and by mastered, I mean shooting scores of 90 or better—you will probably want to move on to one of the smaller guns, such as the .410, 28, or 20-gauge.

Humans are peculiar. No sooner do we master something than we try and make it more challenging. For instance, in golf, we lengthen holes and add hazards; in horse racing, we handicap through weight. And so it is with the game of skeet. As soon as we begin breaking all the targets, we look around for some way to restore the challenge. A smaller gun is the answer. Soon the shooter is either sitting on top of the world because he broke a 97 with the .410 or he's beating his wife and kicking the dog because he broke a 77. It's just as easy to do either one. Unfortunately, there are a lot more 77's than 97's. I think that this is because the shooter either starts with the little gun too soon or fails to understand the problems involved in shooting a smaller gun.

SHOOTING THE .410

Let's take the .410 first. In my opinion it is the only true small-gauge gun. To shoot good scores with the .410, you must first understand the gun itself. The greatest problem in shooting the .410 is not the size of the shot pattern, but the fact that the gun is so hard to control. The point of impact is always the same whether you are shooting a 12-gauge or a .410. However, you must be able to control the point of impact and be able to place it correctly. For a long time this was almost impossible with the .410. The only ones available were the Winchester Model 42 and the Remington Model 11-48. These guns were perfectly capable of breaking all the targets, but we shooters were not capable of controlling the guns to the point of doing the job. This was not all the shooter's fault. The guns were too light, the barrels too small, the stocks too short. We failed to

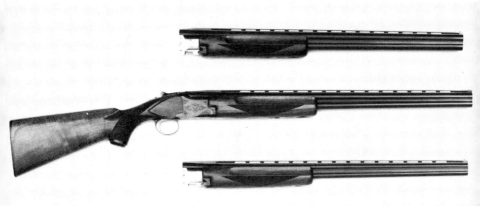

Interchangeable barrels are one answer to the problem of shooting the different gauges. Above is a 20-gauge Model 101 with extra pairs of 28-gauge and .410 barrels.

understand this and were content to win with 95's or 97's. After all, this was what we wanted, a tough little gun to shoot.

But you just can't keep a good man down. First, Ernie Simmons added a ventilated rib, then a larger forearm. Weights were added to the magazine tube and stock. The stock itself was lengthened, and a pistol grip was added. Tubes were made so that it became possible to shoot the .410 shell in a 20- or 12-gauge gun. Suddenly, the problem was gone and along with it, the little gun. What we have now is a large gun shooting a half-ounce load, a gun that is capable of being controlled and one that is almost free of malfunction. No longer can it be referred to as a pea-shooter or an idiot-stick.

When you are ready to move into the .410-gauge, make every effort to get one of the same make as your other guns. Shoot the same type of gun in each event. This is something we couldn't do a few years ago because the guns didn't exist, and it was a great handicap.

Be sure that the stock dimensions are the same as your 12-gauge. The barrel length is not important. Personally, I like to keep it the same as my other guns.

A ventilated rib is a must on the .410, as this adds to the barrel diameter. The larger the barrel, the easier it is to point and keep your eye on both it and the target, not the targets alone. There should be some weight in the front and the back of the gun. One of the greatest disadvantages of the .410 is that it is often made too light, and light guns are uncontrollable. This has been corrected in most of the present-day firearms.

Balance the gun to your liking. Once you have it right, leave it alone. Personally, I do not think that the .410 should weigh as much as the 12-gauge. This not only eliminates the feel of recoil but is apt to lull the shooter into thinking he is shooting a larger gun. Matching your .410 as closely as possible to your 20-gauge is, I think, the perfect answer.

I was once discussing the .410-gauge with a sea captain, Brooksie Thompson, who was the best shot in our area. He said that the best way to shoot the .410 was to go to a shoot, borrow a gun, shoot it, give it back to the man, and then forget it. Well, this no longer holds true. The .410s that we have today are capable of shooting the scores. They're a bit like mules, however; you have to understand them to get them to work.

Shooting a perfect score with any gun is a matter of concentration. Concentration is the ability to get keyed up yet stay relaxed. This is really difficult with the .410. For example, a shooter with a .410 gets to Station 5 without missing and thinks, "All I have to do is to get these and I'll go straight." So he tightens up and immediately misses one. Or, he gets to the same station and he's down three targets, so he starts thinking, if I miss any more, I won't even break 20. So he tightens up and misses again.

The point I'm trying to make is that regardless of which way you shoot with the .410, good or bad, it is hard not to tighten up and try too hard. It is too easy to start counting targets—one more and I'll win, or one more and I'm out. You cannot count targets and retain your confidence and concentration. That is what it takes to shoot the .410—confidence and concentration. And keep them in that order.

You should not start with the .410 too soon. Build up your confidence with the big gun until you can break a poor score without getting upset. Nothing tears down confidence quicker than missing targets, and believe me when I say that you will miss a lot of these with the .410-gauge. Once you are breaking good scores with the 12-gauge you should be able to move into the .410 without getting upset. Just try and stay in the 20's each round. If you try for the perfect score, you will be putting too much pressure on yourself.

Once you have your gun, go out and learn to shoot it. Start with the incomers 1, 2, and 3 and 5, 6, and 7. When you have mastered these, try some outgoers. Shoot the gun just as you would your 12-gauge. Regardless of what a lot of people say, there is very little difference in the apparent-lead picture between the two guns. Remember, the longer the lead, the harder it is to keep the gun moving and stay under the target.

There are five shots where you must be ready—High house 1 and 2, Low house 6 and 7, and both birds at 8. These are non-recovery birds. Your first move has got to be right with the .410. Sometimes it is possible to correct a mistake in one of these stations with the 12-gauge, but not with the .410. So, do your thinking before you call. Pay special attention to High 1, Low 7, and Station 8. These shots probably account for more misses than all of the rest with the little gun. I think this is due to overconfidence by the new shooter and lack of concentration by the experienced shooter. These targets look so much larger in relation to the .410 barrel that if the shooter isn't careful, he is apt to just look at the target. And keep in mind that one of the deceiving targets to shoot with any gun is a straightaway.

I repeat, the gun is capable of breaking all of the targets. All you have to do is teach yourself how to shoot it, physically and mentally. First, you should enjoy shooting the .410. If you do not, then give it up. It will only frustrate you and ruin your 12-gauge scores.

Try not to overestimate your ability. You are not going to shoot the same scores with the little gun as you do with the big one. No one does, not even Barney Hartman. If you can shoot within five and six targets of your 12-gauge score, that is excellent. If you can stay in the 90's with this little gun, you are doing a good job. By keeping this in mind, you can relieve some of the pressure that causes a lot of your misses. You should never walk on the field with the thought of breaking 25 straight with a .410-gauge gun. I say, be happy with 24. Break four 24's and you have a 96. End the season, with a 96 average, there will not be a dozen shooters higher. This way you break a lot of 25's because the pressure is off.

A mistake that a lot of shooters make, especially those of AA and A class, is trying to shoot too fast with a small gun. There is not any advantage in shooting any gun too fast at skeet, especially at incoming targets. Not only do you risk the danger of stopping your swing, but the pattern has not had time to open up to its maximum potential. Actually, you have a lot more time than you think. Why waste it? Take your time and be sure. By all means try and keep your same timing with the .410. Just be ready for the target, get on it, and shoot it when the picture is right, not before.

Practice has been covered earlier in this book. However, I would like to add something here. Don't overdo the practice with the .410-gauge. Over the years I have noticed that the more the shooters practice with the .410, and I mean shooting one round after another, the more confused they get. I find this true in my own shooting. I shoot much better if I practice two rounds with the 12-gauge, then two with the .410. My .410 scores are always better than if I shoot all four rounds with the little gun. Shoot the gun until you have confidence in your ability and the ability of your gun to do what you ask of it. Then shoot only enough to keep sharp.

One more thing before leaving the .410. Too many shooters take the attitude that if they can hit them with the .410, they'll never miss with another gun. Let me tell you, my friend, it does not work that way. The fact that you can drive a little sports car like a professional does not mean that you can handle a ten-wheel truck. Adjust yourself physically and mentally to each gun as if it were the only one you owned. You must be physically able to swing the 12 gauge and mentally able to control the .410. Believe in yourself and have confidence and you can do it.

28-GAUGE

Little need be said about the 28-gauge, as it is just a 20-gauge with a ¾-ounce load. In fact you must be careful that you do not forget and shoot it exactly as you do your 20-gauge. The shot-string is shorter than the 20-gauge, so that you must be a little more careful. Watch incomers on Stations 3 and 5. A long lead is needed here, and if you stop the gun you do not have the shot-string you have in your 20-gauge and 12-gauge to catch the back end of the target.

A great many shooters like to shoot the 28-gauge for

the simple reason that they tell themselves they are shooting a small gun and yet they still shoot a good score with it. As I said earlier, in reality, most 28-gauges are 20-gauge guns with small holes in the barrel. The weight gives them the control and balance they need to break good scores. Over the past 30 years, I doubt if there has been one target difference between my 28-gauge average and my 20-gauge average.

20-GAUGE

In my estimation, this is the perfect skeet gun. It is small enough to be a pleasure and a challenge to shoot, and yet it has the weight, balance, and shot charge to get the job done. It is possible to practice any number of rounds with this gun without getting tired of being banged around by recoil. It is also possible to learn something with it. When you miss, you know what you have done wrong and can correct it. It is a great gun for beginners. It lacks recoil, and it is large enough for the new shooter to hit enough targets to build up his confidence and not get discouraged.

If you are limited to one gun, get a 12-gauge. But, if you can afford two, then get a 20-gauge. If you are a lady or a young shooter, stick with the 20-gauge until you can break your best scores. Then move on up to the 12 and you'll find that you'll pick up four or five targets.

Let me remind you that haste makes waste. Learn to be the best 12- and 20-gauge shooter in the club. Then move on to the smaller guns. Making the move too soon can not only be frustrating but also will do a great deal of damage to your confidence with the other guns.

APPENDIX

THE preceding pages have contained as much about how to "Score Better At Skeet" as I know how to put down on paper, and I hope this information helps you to accomplish your objectives. Aside from skeet-shooting problems themselves, however, the questions I'm asked most frequently do not actually concern skeet shooting proper, but rather, a couple of related topics— how to start a junior off properly in the sport, and the pros and cons of International skeet. So let me add a few words here on these topics for the benefit of those who are interested in them.

When to Start

A subject that is bound to come up in your house sooner or later if you are a dyed-in-the-wool skeet shooter is, "How old should my boy or girl be before I start them shooting?"

Actually, age has very little to do with when they should start. Size and ability to take responsibility are the two controlling factors. Your boy or girl should be large enough to be able to support the gun without leaning back. A boy of only ten may be large enough to hold the gun to his shoulder. On the other hand, I have seen twelve and thirteen-year-old boys who were still too small to start shooting at moving targets. (I say *moving targets*, because if a boy has a desire to shoot, everything possible should be done to keep this desire alive. It is practical for a small boy or girl, using a 13-inch stock, .410-gauge gun with 2½-inch shells, to shoot at clay targets hung on a stake. He will hit enough of these targets to enjoy shooting. At the same time, you will keep his interest alive. He will not feel left out, and there is little danger of hurting his shoulder.)

It's also hard to generalize about responsibility. Some children can assume responsibility at the age of ten, while others are not ready until they are well into their teens. What do I mean by responsibility? Well, if you can send your boy or girl to the store with a list and a ten-dollar bill and know that he will do the job and bring home the change, or if you can leave him to mind a younger child while you run a short errand with full confidence that everything will be all right when you return, I would say that he has reached the point where he can take responsibility. Then, and only then, should the child be given a gun.

All shooting instructions should be done under adult supervision either by yourself or by someone experienced in teaching youngsters. Do not let your eagerness or your child's eagerness override your better judgment. A great deal of harm can be done by starting your boy or girl too soon or too late.

Nothing encourages a young shooter more than break-

Skeet shooting is really a family sport par excellence, provided that supervision and instruction is handled intelligently and the youngsters aren't overmatched at the beginning. The youngest boy here might miss my 85-pound minimum, but in this case skeet seems to run in the family.

ing targets. If he is too small to hold a gun, he will not only miss the target but will probably bruise his shoulder. Do everything possible to keep his interest alive until he is somewhere between ten and twelve years old and weighs about 85 to 100 pounds. Start him out with the right gun, the right way, and it is almost certain that you will come up with another shotgunner in the family, quite possibly one who will pin your ears back at the next registered shoot.

Once you have decided the time is right to start him shooting, be sure you get him the right gun. For young shooters I not only suggest, but insist, on one of the 20-gauge gas-operated automatics. In some cases, where the shooter is very small, the .410-gauge gun can be used to teach position and stance. But as soon as possible, switch to a 20-gauge in order to build his confidence by hitting more targets.

You should use a 20-gauge gas-operated automatic for the following reasons: First, recoil is greatly reduced by the gas operation of the gun. Second, it gives the shooter one less thing to think about when he gets to double shooting. Third, the 20-gauge is light enough for the young shooter to hold and control, yet it throws a large enough pattern to insure hitting enough targets to give him confidence. You already know about confidence—the more he hits, the more confidence he gets; The more confidence he gets the easier it becomes; the easier it becomes, the more he hits.

The .410 gun is lighter, but the percentage of hits will be so small that the shooter soon becomes discouraged. The barrel is also so small that the shooter has a tendency to look at the target and not at the end of the barrel and the target.

Do not let your child talk you into giving him a 12-gauge too soon. This is something they all try to do simply because you shoot a 12-gauge, and they want to be like you. The 12-gauge is so large and heavy that the shooter is constantly trying to hold it by leaning back. This causes the gun to punish him twice as much, and he cannot concentrate on his shots. Every shot becomes an effort, and his shoulder soon becomes bruised.

Let me repeat. Do not let your enthusiasm to create a new shooter or your pupil's desire to become a champion overcome your better judgment by switching him to a 12-gauge gun too soon. From years of teaching I have found that if you start a beginner with a 12-gauge gun, he will reach a certain score and stop; if you start him with a 20-gauge, he will reach the same score, but if you then switch him to a 12-gauge, he will improve four or five targets.

The fit of the gun for the beginner is just as important as it is for you. As soon as possible, have someone who is qualified check the gun to the correct fit. An improperly fitted gun not only gives excess recoil, but also makes the job of learning to shoot twice as hard. Above all, do not push him too hard. I have seen more promising junior shooters ruined by parents who wanted them to excel so badly that they actually finally pushed them out of the game.

Shooting with your boy or girl can make skeet a lot more fun. And that companionship and fun is a lot more important than the trophy. That is coming straight from the horse's mouth, as I have a boy of my own.

International Skeet

In many ways International skeet is simply a return to the game that Davies and Foster originated when they cut their original clock in half. The main exception is that the target is thrown about 11 yards farther, or 71 yards. When the bird is called for the gun must be dismounted from the shoulder—not just visible below the elbow, but touching the hip. The three-second delay on the target is again being reinstated so we are right back where we started in the early twenties. It is true that the target itself is slightly harder in composition, but this was made necessary by the 71-yard distance that it had to be thrown.

International skeet is the only form of skeet shooting recognized by the Olympic committee, which has issued a set of rules for the game. It is also the only kind of skeet shot in foreign countries except for military bases of the United States.

The game is quite a bit more difficult than American skeet, primarily due to the 71-yard target. The speed of this target makes bringing the gun up to the face from a low position both tricky and unpleasant. I am sure that this extreme low gun position on such a fast target has been the reason why International skeet has never become very popular in this country. The shooter is in constant fear that he is going to bang his face with the stock. It is also a very awkward and unnatural way to shoot. It is not a true hunting position, and I'm sure Davies would never have killed a grouse if he had carried his gun in the manner set by the International skeet rules. Nonetheless, it's a challenging game.

If you'd like to try International skeet, the first thing to do is to convince yourself that *on the whole* it is not much harder than regular skeet. However, it *is* different, and adjustments have to be made. For instance, it is not actually any harder to hit your incomers 1, 2, and 3 Low and 5, 6, and 7 High. You have ample time to catch the target. It is still coming at you, perhaps a little faster, but you have to swing faster to catch it. So your apparent lead will increase accordingly if you follow through.

The second thing you must learn is to shoot off the shoulder and on the hip. You must convince yourself that there is no great disadvantage to shooting the gun dismounted. Actually, this is the way the game started and the way the gun was built to be shot. (I've always thought that if the gun was intended to be shot mounted, the designer would have put a rear sight on it.)

Of course, off-the-shoulder shooting is not necessarily on-the-hip shooting. Let me clear up the difference between off-the-shoulder style and shooting of International style. Off-the-shoulder shooters hold the stock approximately three or four inches down from the shoulder so that it is just visible below the elbow. This was also called "dropped stock" shooting in the old days. And this isn't a handicap for the shooter. I'm sure that if the stock position were returned to this distance below the shoulder in International style, you would see about as many 100's shot in that game as there are in our own game of skeet. In International style, the toe of the stock must be resting on the hip bone. This gives a great deal of angle to the gun and poses a definite handicap—it is so far down that it takes a lot of practice to bring it up and seat it in the shoulder pocket correctly without banging the head or snagging the butt on the way up.

Correct International position. The gun butt is touching the top of my hip bone, but other details are only slightly more pronounced than normal: eyes sight directly over the end of the barrel; and position faces well past point at which target will be broken. The left hand is far back on the fore-end to facilitate gun mounting.

Once you decide to shoot International skeet, I suggest that you use a gun with a stock about half an inch shorter than on your regular gun. This will help you get the gun to your shoulder quickly with far less chance of snagging on your shirt or coat. If you use your standard stock, not only will you find it hard to get the gun to your shoulder, but you're going to find your head quite a bit further back on the stock, once you have the gun mounted.

The three-second delay demanded in International skeet will not pose too much of a problem, if you put in a little bit of practice. Just keep telling yourself, "Don't move until you see the target," and you'll soon adjust to this old way of shooting. It will also improve your regular shooting for the simple reason that you teach yourself not to jump the target. Remember, you can never get ahead and wait. You're going to find that you have to break your target later, probably past the target crossing point. So, take a position facing a little more to the right of the one that you have been taking at regular skeet. This will allow for a lot more follow-through, which you are going to need on this fast target.

You can get into all kinds of arguments about choke and shotshell loads to use on International skeet. My advice is to stick to what you've been shooting. Use your same skeet barrel and shoot the three-dram skeet load. This is what you cut your teeth on, and there's no need to change horses in the middle of the stream as far as I'm concerned.

Once you have taken up International skeet, the biggest problem is not going to be the game itself, but finding somewhere to practice, unless you are fortunate enough to live in or near one of those cities that have an International setup. If you can't practice International, you won't be able to shoot International. It's a simple matter to practice low gun and also the three-second delay on almost any range. The 71-yard target is something else, and this is the main problem to the whole game. Most clubs are reluctant to crank the traps up to throw a target this far, and their fears are well-founded. Not only is the motor not geared to pull a spring this heavy, but they're apt to break the housing on the trap itself.

Even with all these drawbacks, there is more International being shot nowadays than ever before. There have been definite efforts to encourage it, and the military teams are required to shoot it. About five years ago, it was introduced into the NSSA World Championship programs. While there is a trend to shoot it today, it is still growing at a relatively slow pace. The reason for this is that people like to do what they can do well and they do well what they enjoy. In my experience, very few people enjoy International skeet. Therefore, very few of them shoot it well.

If you have made up your mind to shoot International skeet, let me give you a word of warning. It is not much of a problem to go from regular skeet to International skeet without upsetting your shooting. But to go from International back to skeet is another problem indeed. The reason is the fast target. If you're not careful, after shooting International you will find yourself in a regular round of skeet way out in front of the target, thus having to stop the gun and wait for it. Your timing will definitely be altered. You're apt to become confused not only on your position but also on your stance, as all of these things change with International shooting.

Before leaving International shooting, let me clear up one subject that turns me on like a red flag does a bull. So many of the shooters and non-shooters who are pushing International skeet claim that regular skeet is a kid's game, or too easy. They insinuate that International skeet shooters are far superior to regular skeet shooters. This is far from true. I know because I put together a list of all the International shooters at the World's Skeet Shoot in Savannah, the last time that it was held there. I checked their scores on the first hundred targets of the all-gauge event. If what we are led to believe is true, they should all have broken 100 X 100 at the easy game of skeet. My friend, I have news for you, only four of those did, and the champion was not among them. The women's champion broke in the low 90's, even though she had broken a 98 in International skeet the day before.

Comparing the two games is like trying to compare grand prix racing with the International 500 at Indianapolis. They are both automobile races. Both are tough and both have great drivers, but it is very seldom that one driver will excel at both events. The International shooters do not do any better at their game than you do at yours. So hold up your head and stick up for your game. But for goodness sake, do not try to force it on the other fellow.

So there you have it—thirty years of shooting experience in a nutshell (or, if you can stand the pun, a shotshell). The only thing I can add, or reemphasize, is that *champions are made, not born.* Don't expect to run before you walk, and don't be disappointed if someone makes faster progress than you do. I don't know anyone who didn't have to work to become a champion, and then work harder to stay there, if only because part of the challenge was gone.

I sure hope that this book has succeeded in fanning some competitive sparks, and hope to see the results on the skeet field. As I've already said, if you need help, don't hesitate to ask—unless, of course, you're shooting scores that fan *my* competitive spark. Then it's every man for himself!

Picture Credits

The author wishes to thank *Skeet Shooting Review* for permission to reproduce the photograph appearing on page 10, Remington Arms Co. for the pictures on pages 6 and 11, and the Winchester-Western Division of Olin Corporation for the pictures on pages 13, 20, 28, 115, 128, 136, 147 and 155. All other pictures were taken by Roy Attaway of Hilton Head Island, S.C. and Gil Tharp of St. Simons Island, Georgia. The line diagrams were executed by George H. Buehler.